Artificial Intelligence, Data and Blockchain in a Digital Economy

First Edition

Singapore University of Social Sciences - World Scientific Future Economy Series

ISSN: 2661-3905

Singapore University of Social Sciences - World Scientific Future Economy Series introduces the new technology trends and challenges that businesses today face, financial management in the digital economy, blockchain technology, smart contract and cryptography. The authors describe current issues that the business leaders and finance professionals are facing, as well as developments in digitalisation. The series covers several increasingly important new areas such as the fourth industrial revolution, Internet of Things (IoT), blockchain technology, artificial intelligence (AI) and many other forces of disruption and breakthroughs that shape today's realities of the economy. A better understanding of the changing environment in the future economy can enable business professionals and leaders to recognise realities, embrace changes, and create new opportunities — locally and globally — in this inevitable digital age.

*Published**

Vol. 3 *Artificial Intelligence, Data and Blockchain in a Digital Economy, First Edition*
edited by David Lee Kuo Chuen, supported by Singapore University of Social Sciences and World Scientific, in support of Singapore Digital (SG:D) and in collaboration with Infocomm Media Development Authority

Vol. 2 *The Emerging Business Models*
by Guan Chong, Jiang Zhiying and Ding Ding

Vol. 1 *AI & Quantum Computing for Finance & Insurance: Fortunes and Challenges for China and America*
by Paul Schulte and David Lee Kuo Chuen

Forthcoming Titles

Financial Management in the Digital Economy
Ding Ding, Guan Chong and David Lee Kuo Chuen

*More information on this series can also be found at
https://www.worldscientific.com/series/susswsfes

(Continued at end of book)

Singapore University of Social Sciences - World Scientific
Future Economy Series 3

Artificial Intelligence, Data and Blockchain in a Digital Economy

First Edition

Edited by
David Lee Kuo Chuen
Singapore University of Social Sciences, Singapore

Supported by
SUSS SINGAPORE UNIVERSITY OF SOCIAL SCIENCES
World Scientific

In support of
SG:D EMPOWERING POSSIBILITIES

In collaboration with
INFOCOMM MEDIA DEVELOPMENT AUTHORITY

Published by

World Scientific Publishing Co. Pte. Ltd.
5 Toh Tuck Link, Singapore 596224
USA office: 27 Warren Street, Suite 401-402, Hackensack, NJ 07601
UK office: 57 Shelton Street, Covent Garden, London WC2H 9HE

National Library Board, Singapore Cataloguing in Publication Data
Name: Lee, David (David Kuo Chuen), editor. | Infocomm Media Development Authority. | Singapore University of Social Sciences.
Title: Artificial intelligence, data and blockchain in a digital economy / edited by David Lee Kuo Chuen.
Description: First edition. | Singapore : World Scientific Publishing Co. Pte. Ltd., [2020] | Series: Singapore University of Social Sciences - World Scientific future economy series ; vol. 3 | Includes bibliographic references and index. | "Supported by Singapore University of Social Sciences, World Scientific, in support of Singapore Digital (SG:D) and in collaboration with Infocomm Media Development Authority".
Identifier(s): OCN 1141872321 | ISBN 978-981-121-994-8 (paperback) | 978-981-121-895-8 (hardcover)
Subject(s): LCSH: Economics--Singapore--21st century. | Technological innovations--Economic aspects--Singapore--21st century. | Artificial intelligence. Blockchains (Databases)--Singapore.
Classification: DDC 330.95957--dc23

British Library Cataloguing-in-Publication Data
A catalogue record for this book is available from the British Library.

For any available supplementary material, please visit
https://www.worldscientific.com/worldscibooks/10.1142/11787#t=suppl

Desk Editors: Anthony Alexander/Yulin Jiang

Typeset by Stallion Press
Email: enquiries@stallionpress.com

About Infocomm Media Development Authority

The Infocomm Media Development Authority (IMDA) leads Singapore's digital transformation with infocomm media. To do this, IMDA will develop a dynamic digital economy and a cohesive digital society, driven by an exceptional infocomm media (ICM) ecosystem — by developing talent, strengthening business capabilities, and enhancing Singapore's ICM infrastructure. IMDA also regulates the telecommunications and media sectors to safeguard consumer interests while fostering a pro-business environment, and enhances Singapore's data protection regime through the Personal Data Protection Commission.

About Singapore University of Social Sciences

The Singapore University of Social Sciences (SUSS) is a university with a rich heritage in providing lifelong, learner-centric and industry-relevant education. Our mission is to champion lifelong education to develop future thinkers and leaders to their fullest potential through our 3H's education philosophy: 'Head', 'Heart', and 'Habit'.

We offer more than 70 undergraduate and graduate programmes, available in full- and part-time study modes which are flexible, modular and multi-faceted in learning experience to cater to both fresh school leavers and adult learners. We also launched for our workforce a broad range of continuing education and modular training courses for professional skills and knowledge upgrade.

Our SUSS FinTech and Blockchain Group bridges the community from the academia and industry to learn from each other on the latest and most relevant topics on FinTech, blockchain and cryptocurrencies, and to explore together the potential of blockchain technology to bring about financial integration and inclusion.

Foreword by Professor David Lee Kuo Chuen

The purpose of this book is to underline Singapore's initiatives in digitalising the nation. More importantly, it introduces different emerging technologies, including AI, and Blockchain and how they are put into practice in service to societies. From this book, you will gather insights on how emerging technologies impact our societies and how Singapore is applying these technologies in different sectors.

SUSS FinTech & Blockchain Group is delighted to partner with IMDA in the publication of this book. It marks the nation's commitment to the digital economy.

This book will be insightful for business practitioners, policymakers and anyone interested in technology and its application. It will be a useful resource for teaching primarily in developing an understanding of how technology is used to better serve mankind.

Professor David Lee Kuo Chuen
Professor, Finance
School of Business
Singapore University of Social Sciences

Acknowledgement

This book is made possible with the contributions of Veronica Tan, Koh Wee Siong and Reynard Neo at IMDA together with faculty members from SUSS including Caroline Lim, Lo Swee Won, Cheryl Wang, Hung Yu-Chen, Ren Jing, who devoted hours in research, coordination, and editorial work.

Contents

Chapter 1

Introduction — Singapore as a Smart Nation

1.1 Overview of Singapore as a Smart Nation[1]

Smart Nation is a transformed Singapore where people will be more empowered to live meaningful and fulfilled lives, enabled seamlessly by technology, that offers exciting opportunities for all. It is where businesses can be more productive and seize new opportunities in the digital economy. It is a nation which collaborates with our international partners to deliver digital solutions and link and benefit people and businesses across boundaries. As Prime Minister Lee described it at the launch of Smart Nation in November 2014, it is a nation where "we can create possibilities for ourselves beyond what we imagined possible."

Smart Nation is integral to Singapore's next phase of nation building. To continue to prosper and stay relevant in the world, Singapore needs to ride the waves of the digital revolution and capture the opportunities it brings, just as we embraced globalisation before. Digitalisation presents opportunities for Singapore to enhance Singapore's traditional strengths, address and overcome our national challenges and physical limits, be it resource constraints or an ageing population, as well as build new sources of comparative advantage for Singapore. This new era of digital transformation will power Singapore to SG100 and beyond.

---

[1] *"Smart Nation: The Way Forward"*, Smart Nation and Digital Government Office, November 2018.

To achieve Smart Nation, we start from a position of strength, riding on Singapore's early investments in technology and connectivity infrastructure, and strong institutions that are ready to seize these opportunities. Our people are also digitally literate, with a strong pool of talent who perform well in the STEM (Science, Technology, Engineering, and Mathematics) disciplines.

1.2 A Brief History of Singapore's National Digitalisation Efforts

Singapore has done this before. In our history, we have undergone two successful whole-of-nation transformations in response to digital disruption. First, with National Computerisation from the 1980s to early-1990s, to transform Singapore into a regional centre for computer software development and services. Second, with the growth of the info-communications industry from the mid-1990s to early 2010s, to transform Singapore into a hyper-networked, global hub for services.

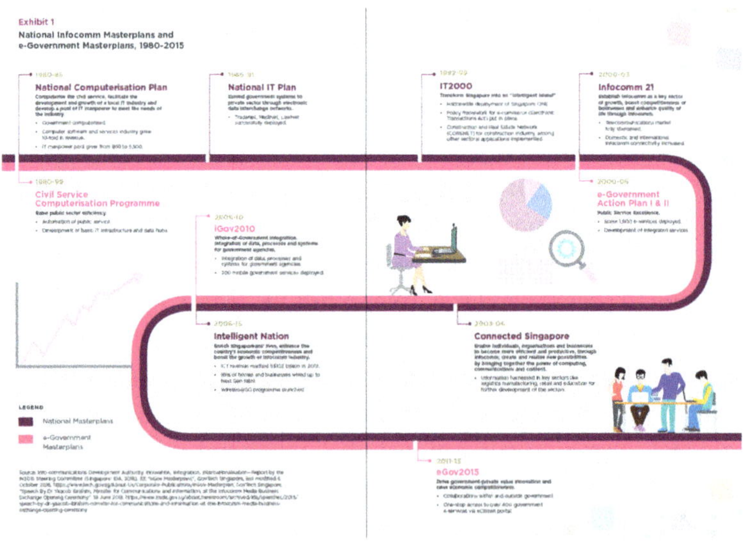

Figure 1.1. National Infocomm Masterplans and e-Government Masterplans, 1980–2015.

Source: Centre for Liveable Cities.

It was in the early 1980s that the Government recognised computerisation as an essential tool for competing with the rest of the world, and mobilised the nation to embrace new technology. Since then, six national Info-communications Technology (ICT) masterplans have been launched (see Figure 1.1). In the formative years, the focus was to computerise government agencies and drive up the quality and number of IT professionals in Singapore. Subsequent masterplans focused on extending computerisation and connectivity to the private sector.

While each masterplan had a different emphasis to address challenges of the period, the underlying objectives have been clear and consistent — to guide the use of ICT to enhance Singapore's international competitiveness, upgrade the skills of citizens especially the workforce, improve service standards, and attract knowledge-intensive activities.

1.3 What a Smart Nation Would Look Like

Today, Singapore is at another pivotal moment in its digital transformation journey (see Figure 1.2). The pace of technological invention and innovation is accelerating at an unprecedented rate, and we must do better to fully harness this power and potential to improve lives and create opportunities.

Our Smart Nation journey endeavours to transform Singapore through technology. Technology is only a means to an end, to enable significant improvements in how we live, work, and play. We cannot simply apply the latest technologies on top of our existing processes and organisations. It

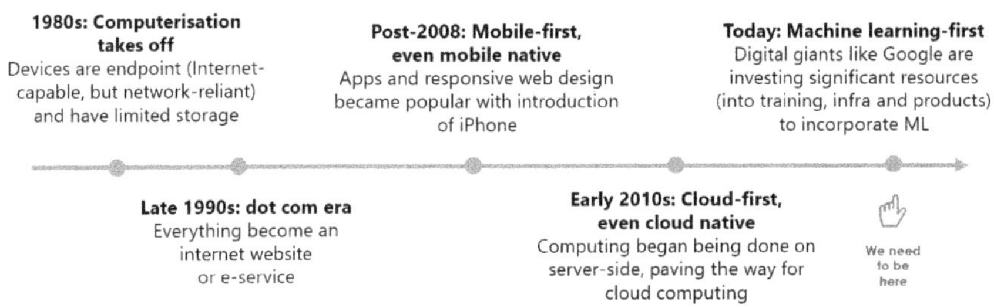

Figure 1.2. Digital Transformation Journey.

Source: Smart Nation and Digital Government Office.

will require a fundamental rethink of our long-held assumptions and how we operate.

As a nation and city-state, Singapore's Smart Nation initiative is unique among the efforts of many other smart cities. Singapore's single layer of Government not only seeks to improve city and municipal services through technology, but has the capacity to drive transformation at the national scale. At a national level, we are able to drive economic and civic engagement, as well as enable efficient and effective planning and administration. At the same time, we can drive transformation in critical areas such as energy management, national security, trade, and foreign relations. We are able and ready to make bold changes that will improve all aspects of our people's lives.

Our priority is to harness technology to address national challenges and drive transformation in key domains: health, education, transport, urban solutions, and finance.

- **Health:** Our healthcare system will move beyond healthcare to health, as Singaporeans will be better equipped and empowered to take care of their own health. Healthcare services, where they are needed, will be delivered efficiently. Singaporeans are already using wearable devices or smartphones to monitor their health and activities, and this data can empower individuals and inform service delivery.
- **Education:** Digital technology unlocks a new realm of self-directed and collaborative learning. Relationships between students, teachers, and parents, as well as capabilities of the physical infrastructure are augmented to create a holistic and conducive environment for effective learning. Routine and repetitive tasks are automated to help educators focus on the work that matters. In the long run, we will need to rethink our philosophies, content, and modality of learning as technology evolves.
- **Transport:** Data analytics, smart systems, and autonomous vehicles are key solutions for the future of transport planning and operations. Our roads and transport system will be optimised, making traffic smoother, public transport more comfortable and reliable, and the air cleaner with less need for private cars.

- **Urban Solutions:** Our homes and estates will be safer, more comfortable, and more sustainable. The use of sensors and smart systems will improve the effectiveness of municipal services, save energy, and ensure sustainable use of resources.
- **Finance:** Singapore will continue to be a leading regional and global financial hub, powered by financial institutions that readily adopt fintech solutions for better customer service, greater efficiencies in trade finance, strengthened supervision, and reduced compliance cost.

At its core, Smart Nation is about empowering our people. Understandably, there might be some fears and tensions about technology destabilising livelihoods, raising costs, and increasing vulnerabilities. However, if we identify these challenges and tackle them head on, technology can result in better jobs and business opportunities, more security, and improvement of livelihoods.

Everyone is part of Smart Nation, and will be better equipped to imagine, design, and implement, as well as enjoy the opportunities and conveniences of a digital society. This means having the means to transact digitally, the skills and confidence to use technology, and the agility to adapt to change and keep up with the latest technologies to achieve a better quality of life, as well as contribute to innovations in the digital era. This will put us in good stead for an ever-changing global environment.

Smart Nation is for Singapore and Singaporeans. It requires a whole-of-nation effort, involving every Government agency, every business, and also our people. The Government will take responsibility for the digital transformation of Government functions and services, and businesses must step up to transform and keep up with the winds of technological change. At the same time, Government will partner the civil society to drive the digital readiness and harness technology for stronger social cohesion.

1.4 Becoming a Smart Nation

Singapore has laid out mutually-reinforcing plans to build a **Digital Economy, Digital Government** and **Digital Society**, involving the public, private, and people sectors. This means every industry, business, and government agency stepping up to accelerate its digitalisation efforts, to build capabilities and solutions that will propel the nation forward. This whole-of-nation movement will be powered by a society of digitally ready citizens and communities, confident and eager to learn about and adopt digital technologies.

The government has outlined broad plans to transform our Economy, Government and Society through the Digital Economy Framework for Action, Digital Government Blueprint, and the Digital Readiness Blueprint. A Digital Government will provide the environment and drive enablers to shape the Digital Economy and a Digital Society. A Digital Economy will work closely with Digital Government to support the digitalisation of Government service delivery and build industry capability for future transformation needs. We are also doing further work to develop a holistic approach to cultivate a Digital Society which is confident to harness technology.

1.4.1 *Digital Economy*

Going digital is a national imperative for a better future for Singaporeans. Digitalisation is about enabling new possibilities across the economy, with business growth and better jobs. Grasping these opportunities will allow Singapore to develop new comparative advantages and remain a smart and thriving nation that continually attracts investments and talents to her shores. The Singapore Digital (SG:D) movement was launched to spur our digitalisation efforts, with the Government, companies, organisations, and individuals to reap the benefits of a digital economy. Our vision is to be a leading digital economy that continually reinvents itself in the fourth industrial revolution.

We do this via accelerating the digital transformation of existing economic sectors, fostering new ecosystems enabled by digital technologies, and developing a next-generation digital industry in sectors

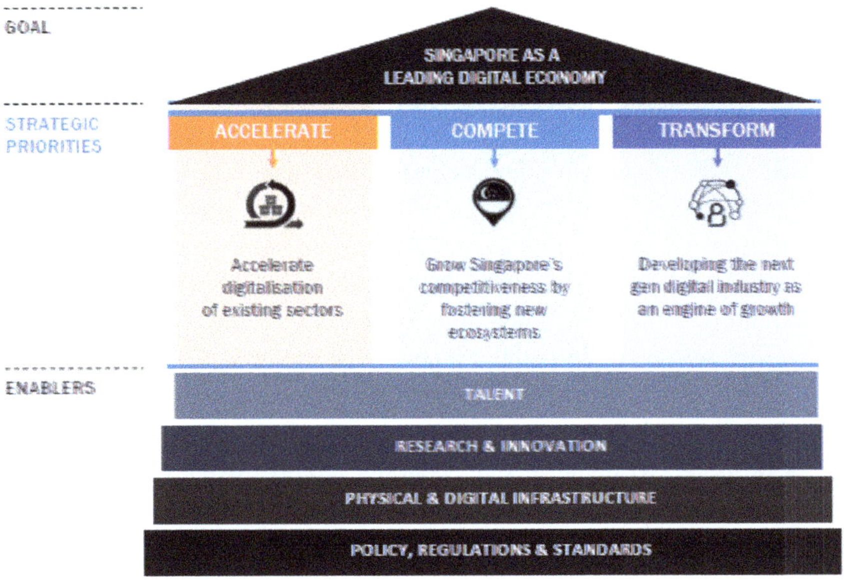

Figure 1.3. The Digital Economy Framework for Action.

Source: Infocomm Media Development Authority.

such as cybersecurity as an engine of growth. This is outlined in the Digital Economy Framework for Action by the Infocomm Media Development Authority (IMDA) (see Figure 1.3).

The Digital Economy Framework for Action has three key strategic priorities:

- **Accelerate:** To accelerate the digitalisation of our existing industries for productivity improvements, efficiency gains, and new revenue opportunities. The Committee of Future Economy had rolled out 23 Industry Transformation Maps (ITMs) in 2017 and along these ITMs are Industry Digital Plans to facilitate digitalisation in selected industries. The SMEs Go Digital programme helps to make the transition to digital simpler for SMEs. The Industry Digital Plans for SMEs (IDPs), which are aligned to the ITMs, provide SMEs with step-by-step guidance on the digital technologies to use at each stage of their growth — SMEs can self-assess their digital readiness, seek advice on their digitalisation journey, deploy curated solutions, participate in industry-led pilot projects, and engage project management services to implement their digital projects. IMDA is also working with businesses and government agencies on impactful projects that can accelerate the pace of digital change for industry sectors. These include innovative concepts in urban logistics such as federated lockers for more convenient last mile delivery, the Kampong Glam precinct-level transformation, and the Punggol Digital District which will be a vibrant and inclusive district underpinned by cutting edge technology and a hub for key growth sectors of the Digital Economy.

- **Compete:** To enhance our economic competitiveness by fostering new integrated ecosystems converged around customers' needs. With the blurring of sector boundaries in today's economy, consumers can increasingly dictate how products and services are designed and delivered around their needs, resulting in the formation of new business ecosystems and market intermediaries. These new ecosystems will form the foundation of future industries. Singapore aims to foster a conducive environment for the growth of such integrated ecosystems and support our businesses to innovate and evolve their business models, and become competitive in the global marketplace. The Open Innovation Platform (OIP), a structured innovation process, facilitates collaboration between problem owners and Infocomm Media (ICM) companies to accelerate the development of innovative, new, and scalable solutions that address real business problems.
- **Transform:** To develop the next generation digital industry as an engine of growth for the economy, and a driver of digitalisation across all industries. IMDA wants to transform the ICM industry to be a key growth driver of Singapore's digital economy, and a driver of digitalisation across all industries. IMDA will be building deep capabilities in four frontier technology sectors — Data Science and Artificial Intelligence (AI), Cybersecurity, Immersive Media, Internet of Things (IOT) and Future Communications Infrastructure. The Accreditation@SG:D aims to level the playing field for promising Singapore-based technology companies to win projects, grow and

compete in the global market by helping them establish their credentials, and facilitating access to Government and large enterprise buyers. Accredited companies are thus better-recognised overseas with a trusted Singapore branding and the Singapore Government will also facilitate overseas growth of Singapore companies through targeted programmes for Singapore enterprises. The Singapore Economic Development Board, Enterprise Singapore, and IMDA will jointly lead engagement with leading digital companies globally and groom Singapore-based digital companies, to create good jobs, accelerate the building of capabilities, and encourage technology collaborations in our local ecosystem. Four cross-cutting enablers will also support these pillars of growth:

- **Talent:** To continually upskill, re-skill, and raise the digital capabilities of the workforce.
- **Research and Innovation:** For firms to innovate and leverage intellectual property for competitive advantage, harnessing the capabilities in our research and innovation community.
- **Policy, Regulations and Standards:** To ensure that our policy and regulatory environment, including the environment for data innovation, is globally competitive in a digital world.
- **Physical and Digital Infrastructure:** To ensure that connectivity, platforms, data, and other infrastructure support the growth of the digital economy.

1.4.2 *Digital Government*

The Singapore Government endeavours to build leaner and stronger public agencies which are digital to the core, at the global leading edge of service delivery, transformation, and innovation. The Government will empower public servants to continue to serve with heart, commanding strong public trust, confidence, and support. Outlining the strategies and desired outcomes for this transformation is the Digital Government Blueprint by the Smart Nation and Digital Government Group (see Figure 1.4).

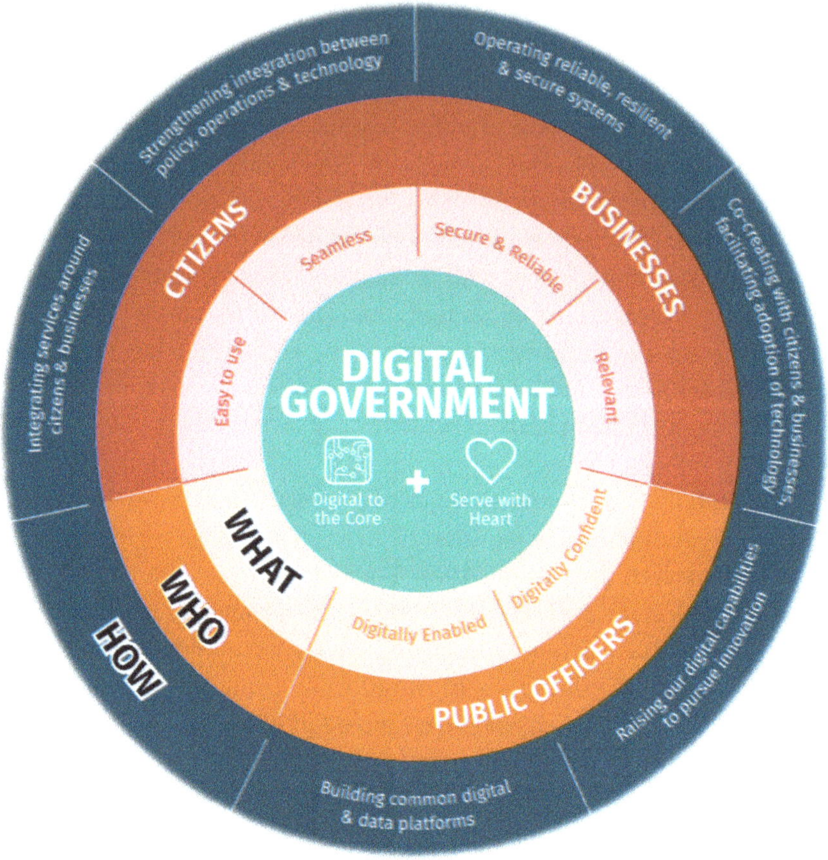

Figure 1.4. Digital Government Blueprint.

Source: Digital Government Blueprint, Smart Nation, and Digital Government Office.

The Digital Government Blueprint is only the first statement of intent to enable a public service that is leaner and stronger, with skilled and adaptable officers at the leading edge of service delivery and innovation. The Singapore Government is moving towards the ability to leverage data, cloud computing, and common digital services and infrastructure. Steps taken include developing a Government Data Strategy and Government Data Architecture to enable sharing of core government datasets in less than 10 days, shifting less sensitive systems to commercial cloud, and building a Singapore Government Tech Stack available to all government agencies to build their digital applications. The Government is making strategic bets in frontier technologies like AI to ensure its digital and physical systems are intelligent to the core. This re-engineering of the technical infrastructure will allow the Government to more efficiently and effectively collaborate with the people and private sectors to deliver policies and services. At the same time, the Government is committed to continually safeguard both Government and citizens' data, and ensure that critical public services remain unaffected. Internally, the Government is also rethinking its manpower and workforce strategies to grow its technology talent pool, incentivise for excellence, and upskill public officers with data science and AI capabilities. The Digital Government Blueprint also sets out bold targets to be achieved by 2023 (see Figure 1.5).

1.4.3 *Digital Society*

In a Smart Nation, Singaporeans are empowered to maximise the opportunities and leverage conveniences of a digital society to lead meaningful lives. The Government will support this by making our services more accessible, raising our people's digital literacy, and encouraging people to participate in digital communities and platforms. To support this, the Ministry of Communications and Information has introduced a Digital Readiness Blueprint (see Figure 1.6).

The Digital Readiness Blueprint was written with inputs from the people and private sectors, sets out recommendations for building Singapore's Digital Readiness, guided by four strategic trusts, namely:

- Expand and Enhance Digital Access for Inclusivity.
- Infuse Digital Literacy into the National Consciousness.
- Empower Community and Businesses to Drive Widespread Adoption of Technology.
- Promote Digital Inclusion by Design.

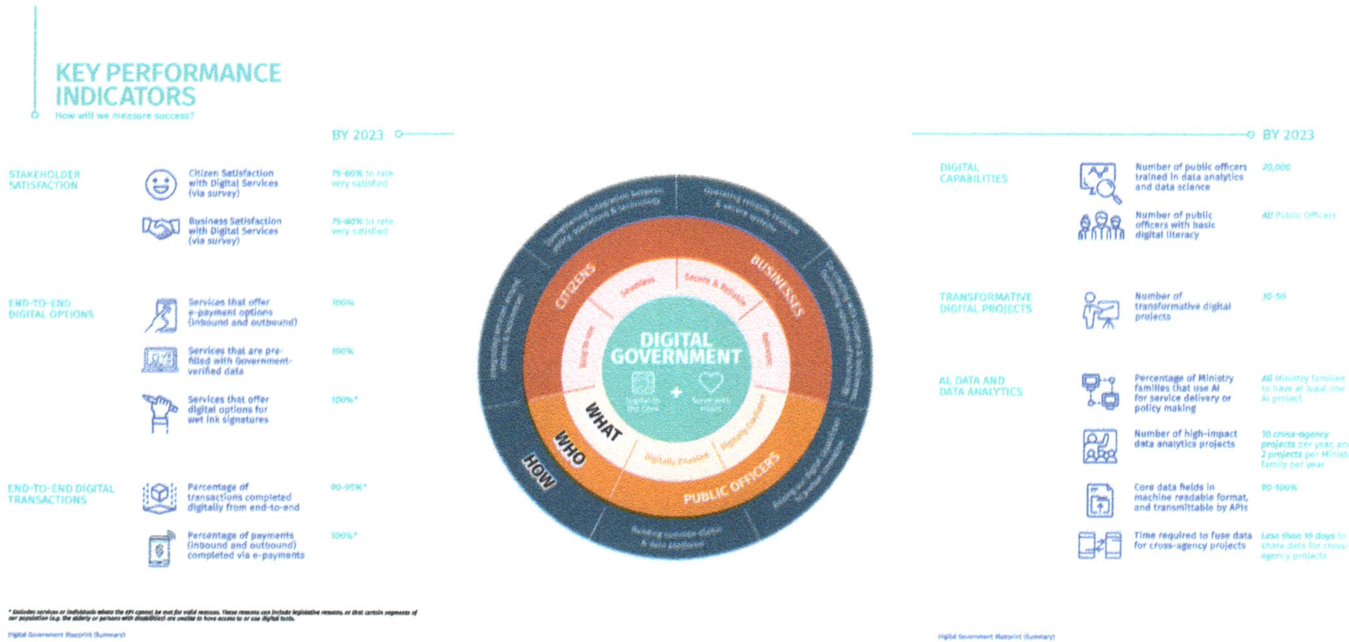

Figure 1.5. The Digital Government Blueprint Targets.

Source: Digital Government Blueprint, Smart Nation and Digital Government Office.

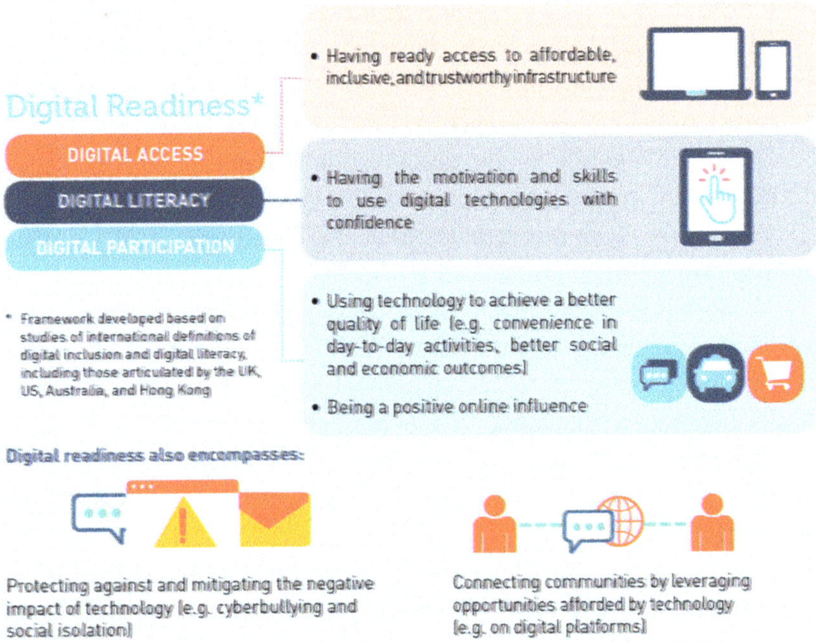

Figure 1.6. Digital Readiness Blueprint.

Source: Ministry of Communications and Information.

Guided by the above, the blueprint offers 10 recommendations:

- Make access to basic digital enablers as widespread as possible.
- Customise access packages for those with specific needs.
- Identify a set of basic digital skills for everyday activities to spur take-up of digital technology, especially among the less digitally savvy.
- Strengthen focus on information and media literacy to build resilience in an era of online falsehoods.
- Ensure that our children and youth grow up to form meaningful relationships with people around them and use technology to benefit their communities.
- Encourage private and people sector organisations to amplify efforts and help more Singaporeans adopt technology.

- Provide one-on-one assistance to make it easy for Singaporeans to adopt technology, especially those who find it challenging.
- Provide support for projects that create opportunities for community participation.
- Encourage organisations to design for inclusion.
- Reach out to more Singaporeans by ensuring that relevant digital services are made available in vernacular languages.

As more public and private sector services go digital, the people will also increase their digital behaviours. While there are fears and anxieties surrounding the use of technology, the speed at which we become a Digital Society is dependent on how quickly we are able to adapt. We must recognise how daily digital behaviour contributes to better policy insights and service delivery, and actively work towards being digital individuals.

At the same time, rapid developments in digital technologies will also have an impact on our society. Technology has the potential to influence where individuals spend their time and bring communities together to support causes. A Digital Society will need to take into account how technology can unite rather than divide, and how society as a whole can be more resilient and adaptable to changes. Hence, building upon the Digital Readiness Blueprint, the Government will develop a holistic approach to build a Digital Society.

1.5 What's Next in Our Smart Nation Journey?

Over the past five years, Singapore has made clear progress towards our Smart Nation and Digital Government vision. The Public Service is now clearer about its transformation mission and what success would look like by 2023 (as reflected in the Digital Government Blueprint). Our companies are embracing digital technologies and beginning their own digital transformation journeys. More people are learning about technology, whether in schools or through online learning.

The Smart Nation journey is an ongoing and ever-evolving one. Our Smart Nation strategy must be developed and implemented iteratively, to enable us to be responsive to a rapidly changing technology landscape and to seize new opportunities. AI, as a general purpose technology, represents the next key frontier of technological opportunities that cuts across all sectors and applications, with both deep and wide impact for Singapore. To harness the full potential of AI and power the next bound of our economic growth, we have formed an interagency team to develop a National AI Strategy — this represents the next bound of our Smart Nation efforts, and builds on the data and digitalisation foundations that we are putting in place today.

Ultimately, Smart Nation is about harnessing technology to stay ahead as a global city and to improve lives and livelihoods for all. It requires a whole-of-nation effort, and we must come together to write the next chapter of the Singapore Story.

Chapter 2

Technology Study on Artificial Intelligence, Data and Blockchain

2.1 Introduction

Digital transformation continues to disrupt how business operate, create new growth opportunities for businesses, and improve the lives of citizens. To help business seize these opportunities from emerging technologies, there is a need to have a better grasp of major technology trends, understand their implications, and respond boldly and nimbly. IMDA published the Services and Digital Economy (SDE) Technology Roadmap[1] to provide a view of the digital technology landscape over the next three to five years. The technology areas outlined include Artificial Intelligence (AI) and Data, and Blockchain, Future Communications & IoT, Immersive Media & Advance Interfaces, Cyber Security and Future-Ready Systems, which give our enterprises and workforce the competitive edge in a digital economy.

This book elaborates on the technology roadmap developed for AI, data and blockchain.

2.2 Market Study

2.2.1 *Overview*

AI has consistently been cited as one of the key technology areas with the potential to affect every aspect of the digital world, and is also one of the

[1] *"Services and Digital Economy (SDE) Technology Roadmap"*, IMDA, November 2018.

four frontier technology focus areas identified by IMDA to lay a strong infocomm media foundation for Singapore.[2] McKinsey Global Institute suggests that AI has the potential to deliver additional global economic activity of around US$13 trillion by 2030, or about 16% higher cumulative GDP compared with today. This amounts to 1.2% additional GDP growth per year.[3]

Prior to 2018, AI was primarily in the domain of large technology companies that deployed machine learning to increase efficiency and scale, but in 2019, AI started showing signs of being more ubiquitous.[4] Gartner's 2019 CIO survey indicated that the number of enterprises implementing AI grew 270% in the past four years and tripled in the past year.[5]

Blockchain, on the other hand, is still in the early phase of adoption. Gartner's 2019 CIO Agenda Survey indicates that of more than 3,000 CIOs surveyed, only 11% indicated they have deployed or are in short-term planning with blockchain.[6] However, industry sentiment for blockchain in the longer-term is still bullish, with projections that suggest that blockchain technology will create more than US$176 billion worth of business value by 2025 and US$3.1 trillion by 2030.[7]

2.2.2 *Global Market Potential of AI*

2.2.2.1 *Economic Opportunities*

The Accenture report "Why Artificial Intelligence is the Future of Growth", suggested that AI has the potential to double annual economic growth in the following countries analysed in terms of gross value added (a close approximation of GDP) (see Figures 2.1 and 2.2):

---

[2] *"Four Frontier Technology are Identified for Development in Singapore"*, IMDA, 2018.

[3] *"Notes from the AI Frontier: Modeling the Impact of AI on the World Economy"*, McKinsey Global Institute, September 2018.

[4] *"The Growth and Potential of AI"*, Forbes, February 2019.

[5] *"Gartner Survey Shows 37 Percent of Organisations have Implemented AI in Some Form"*, Gartner, January 2019.

[6] *"Gartner Reveals Seven Mistakes to Avoid in Blockchain Projects"*, Gartner, June 2019.

[7] *"Gartner: Blockchain will Deliver $3.1 Trillion Dollars in Value by 2030"*, ConsenSys, June 2019.

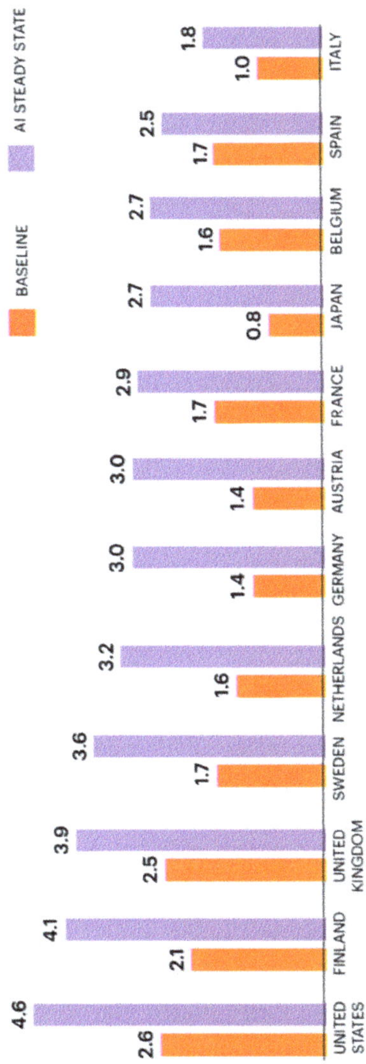

Figure 2.1. Economic Impact of AI: Real Gross Value Added (GVA), (%, Growth).

Source: *"Why Artificial Intelligence is the Future of Growth"*, Accenture, 2016.

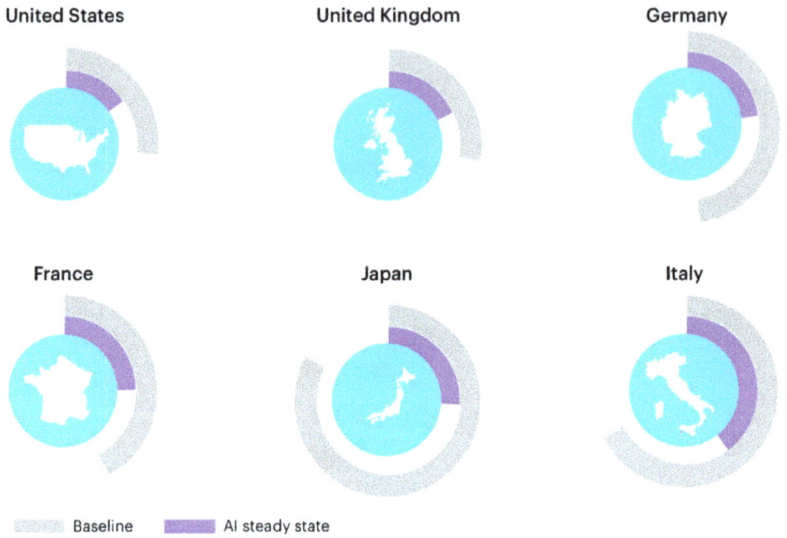

Figure 2.2. Economic Impact of AI — Number of Years for the Economy to Double in Size (A Full Circle Represents 100 Years).

Source: *"Why Artificial Intelligence is the Future of Growth"*, Accenture, 2016.

Since then, other projections have been released to project the impact of AI on the global economy. The McKinsey report, "Modeling the Impact of AI on the World Economy"[8] suggests that AI could add around 16% to global output by 2030, or about US$13 trillion, compared with today. McKinsey's analysis is premised on seven possible channels of impact. As shown in Figure 2.3, the first three relate to the impact of AI adoption on the need for, and mix of, production factors that have direct impact on the productivity of firms. The other four are externalities linked to the adoption of AI and related to the broad economic environment and the transition to AI.

Given the economic potential of AI to uplift economies, and analysis that indicate that AI adoption could widen gaps between countries (e.g. late adopters finding it difficult to generate impact from AI, because front-runners have already captured AI opportunities and late adopters lag in

[8] *"Modeling the Impact of AI on the World Economy"*, McKinsey Global Institute, September 2018.

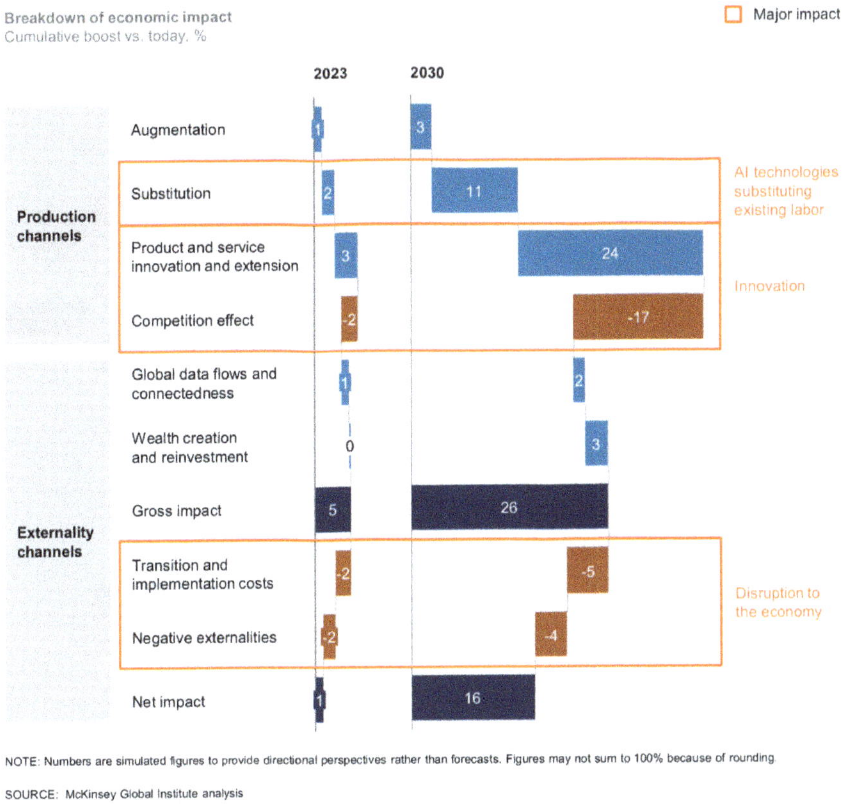

Figure 2.3. AI's Net Economic Impact Based on Seven Dimensions.

Source: *"Modeling the Impact of AI on the World Economy"*, McKinsey Global Institute, September 2018.

developing capabilities and attracting talent),[9] countries around the world are in a "tech arms race",[10] with many countries launching national AI strategies. Singapore launched its National AI Strategy[11] with the vision

---

[9] *"Notes from the AI Frontier: Modeling the Impact of AI on the World Economy"*, McKinsey Global Institute, September 2018.
[10] *"The New Tech Arms Race: A Review of National AI Strategies"*, EnterpriseIoTInsights.com, April 2018.
[11] *"National Artificial Intelligence Strategy, Smart Nation and Digital Government Office"*, April 2020.

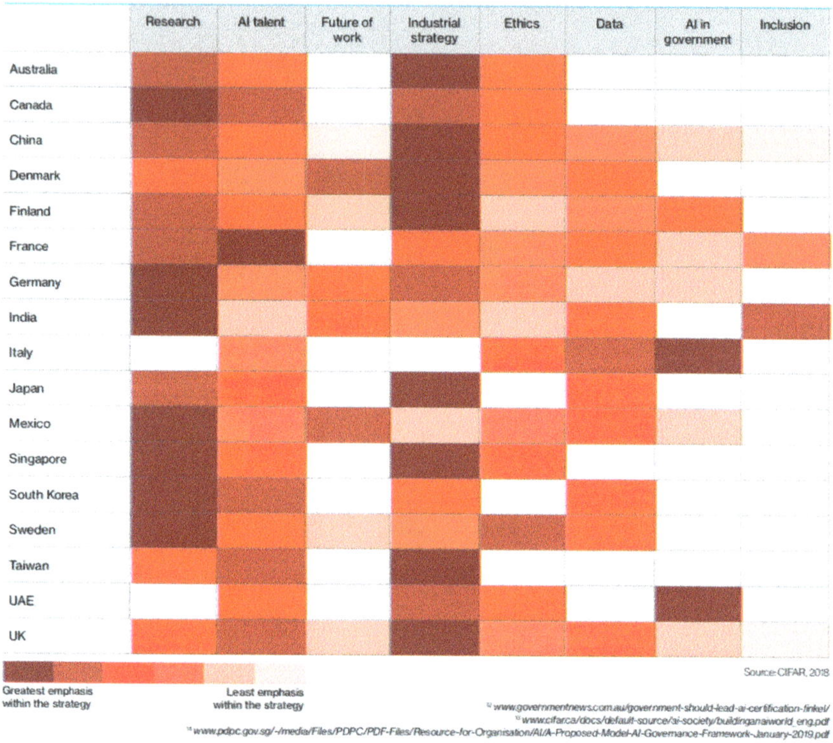

Figure 2.4. National AI Strategies and Priority Areas.

Source: *"Asia's AI Agenda: The Ethics of AI"*, MIT Technology Review, July 2019.

to be a leader in developing and deploying scalable, impactful AI solutions by 2030.

Examples of national AI strategies and their areas of priority are shown in Figure 2.4.

2.2.2.2 *Sector Opportunities and Adoption*

Sector-by-sector adoption of AI is highly uneven as in Figure 2.5, with AI adoption occurring faster in more digitalised sectors and across the value chain:

The "Intelligent Economies: AI's Transformation of Industries and Society" report by the Economist Intelligent Unit provides insights on the more frequently used AI technologies such as image analysis and virtual

Foreword by Mr Philip Heah

Assistant Chief Executive, Technology & Infrastructure Group
Infocomm Media Development Authority (IMDA)

As part of effort to drive Singapore's Digital Economy, the Infocomm Media Development Authority (IMDA), in consultation with industry, developed the Services and Digital Economy Technology Roadmap in 2018. This roadmap helped to identify key shifts and trends in technologies such as Artificial Intelligence (AI), Blockchain and Data over the next three to five years.

I am pleased to announce that IMDA, in collaboration with the Singapore University of Social Sciences (SUSS), have jointly published the *Artificial Intelligence, Data and Blockchain in a Digital Economy, First Edition*.

Listed as one of the frontier technology focused area identified by IMDA, AI will help to lay a strong infocomm media foundation for Singapore. IMDA's Model AI Governance Framework, first released in 2019, has facilitated private sector enterprise AI deployments, through readily implementable guidelines on how to address key ethical and governance issues.

Other frontier technologies such as Blockchain also have the potential to enhance Singapore's digital competitiveness in this vibrant and evolving ecosystem. IMDA had since led a series of programmes to catalyse the development of the Singapore blockchain ecosystem such as OpenNodes. Other exciting developments include the Singapore

Blockchain Ecosystem Report, co-developed by IMDA, Monetary Authority of Singapore and Temasek, to provide an overview representation of the Singapore's vibrant and diverse blockchain landscape.

The *Artificial Intelligence, Data and Blockchain in a Digital Economy, First Edition*, will build on the Services and Digital Economy Technology Roadmap and provide valuable insights on transformative services and how the convergence of technologies. This will help to provide economic growth for Singapore, new growth opportunities for businesses and improve the lives of citizens.

I would like to take this opportunity to thank SUSS for its contribution for the timely push of this publication. We look forward to working closely with more industry partners, institutes of higher learning and other government agencies in helping companies transform in Singapore's Digital Economy.

Mr Philip Heah
Assistant Chief Executive, Technology & Infrastructure Group
Infocomm Media Development Authority (IMDA)

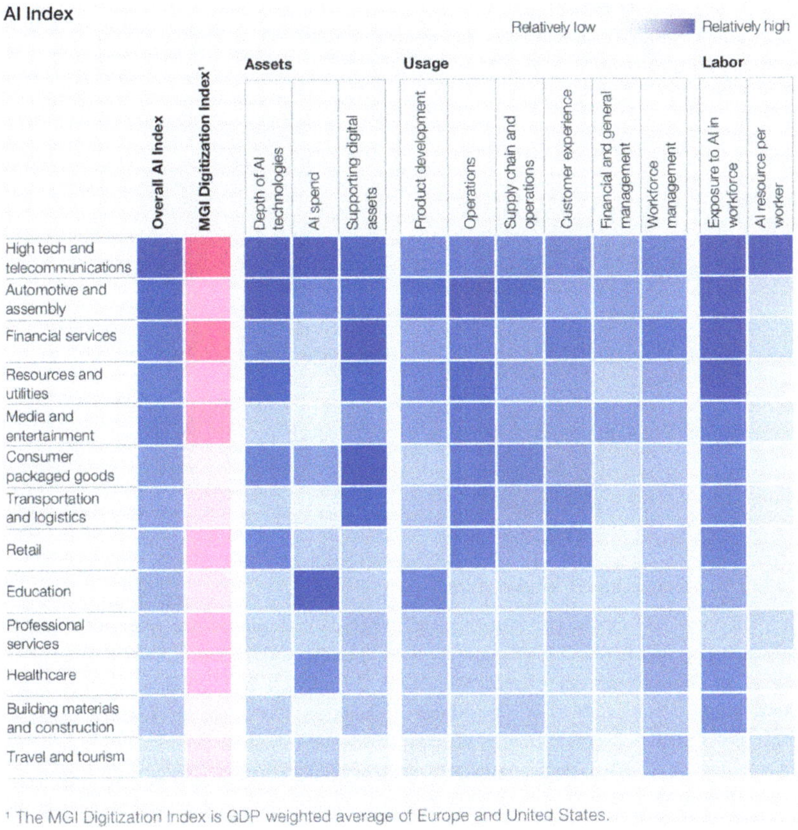

Figure 2.5. Sector-by-Sector Adoption of AI.

Source: *"Driving Impact at Scale from Automation and AI"*, McKinsey Global Institute, February 2019.

assistants, as well as top AI use cases in enterprises such as predictive analytics and real-time operations management.[12]

2.2.3 *Singapore Market Potential of AI*

For Singapore, the AI market has the potential to become a US$960 million market in 2022 and US$16 billion by 2030 with a Compound Annual

[12] *"Intelligent Economies: AI's Transformation of Industries and Society"*, Economist Intelligent Unit, 2019.

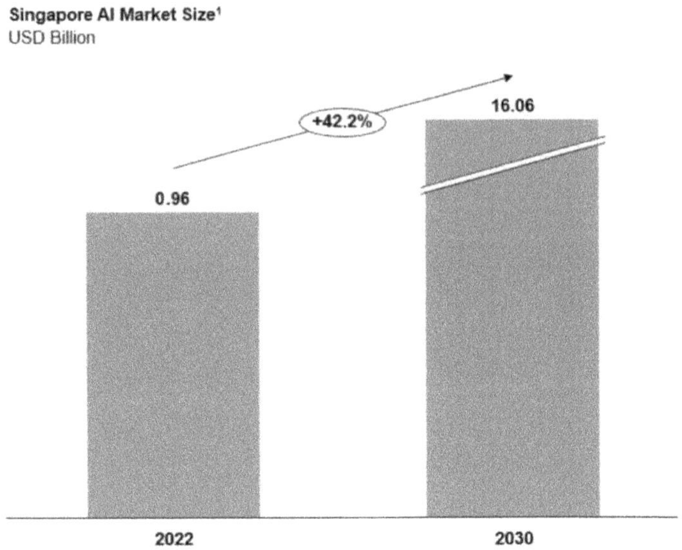

Figure 2.6. Singapore AI Market Size.

Note: [1]Singapore's AI market size is triangulated based on data and insights from: IDC Worldwide Semiannual Cognitive Artificial Intelligence Systems Spending Guide; Gartner Forecast: Enterprise IT Spending by Vertical Industry Market, Worldwide, 2016–2022, 2Q18 Update; Gartner Forecast: Communications Service Provider Operational Technology, Worldwide by Country, 2016–2022; Gartner Broadband Access Systems by Region, 1998–2007; Gartner Consumer Communications Market Revenue 2007–2013; "Welcome to 2018, the year of AI", Microsoft Asia News, 3 January, 2018.

Growth Rate (CAGR) of 42.2%.[13] This includes a wide range of technologies used to "analyse, organise, access and provide advisory services based on a range of unstructured information",[14] as indicated by Figure 2.6.

[13]The market forecast for AI and Blockchain is based on the S-Curve. The S-Curve is a mathematical model which produces highly quantitative results, and is applied to various fields such as physics, biology, and economics. It is a meaningful model which reflects natural law, and is widely used to analyse specific technologies. The S-Curve is helpful in measuring technological growth at each stage of the life cycle (initial adoption, growth, maturity, and decline), and for predicting the time frame of each life cycle. Hence, by identifying where a technology is at on the S-curve, its future growth and potential can be predicted.

[14]*"The 3rd Platform Is Evolving"*, IDC: The Premier Global Market Intelligence Company.

2.2.4 *Global Market Potential of Blockchain*[15]

2.2.4.1 *Economic Opportunities*

Unlike AI, blockchain is relatively less mature in the diffusion of innovation curve (see Figure 2.7). Blockchain has been described as being at the phase of the "early majority" for investments, however, in the technology aspects of blockchain, it is still in the "early adopter", or perhaps in the "innovator" stage.[16]

Gartner's 2019 CIO Agenda Survey indicates that of more than 3,000 CIOs surveyed, only 11% indicated they have deployed or are in short-term planning with blockchain.[17]

However, there is acknowledgement that blockchain technologies offer a set of capabilities that provide for new business and computing paradigms. *Forbes* highlights the key value proposition of blockchain technology — that trust is a fundamental element of business transactions when two parties engage in an agreement to exchange value, however, building trust between two parties comes at a cost, and the trust problem can be resolved by blockchain as it guarantees an immutable transaction with no need for intermediary institutions that would take a cut or delay the transaction.[18]

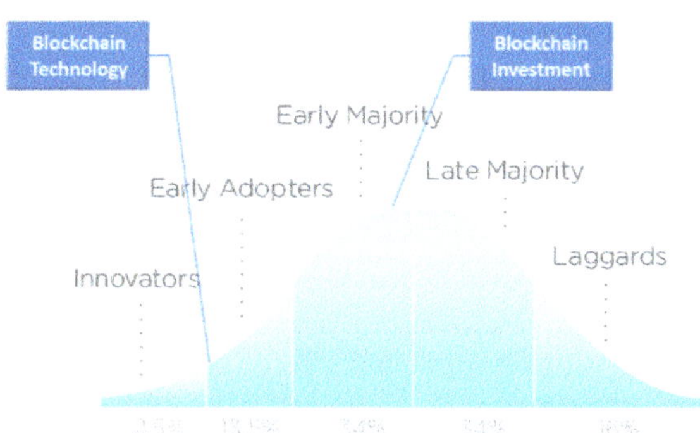

Figure 2.7. Blockchain in the Diffusion of Innovation Curve.

Source: *"Technology Life Cycle"*, Wikipedia.

[15] Includes other distributed ledger technologies.

[16] *"Blockchain Adoption: How Close are We Really?"* Forbes, January 2018.

[17] *"Gartner Reveals Seven Mistakes to Avoid in Blockchain Projects"*, Gartner, June 2019.

[18] *"The Bitcoin Hype and the Potential Disruptive Power of Blockchain"*, Forbes, February 2018.

Figure 2.8. Adoption of Foundational Technologies Like Blockchain.

Harvard Business Review suggests that blockchain is a foundational technology, and adoption is expected to take place in four phases as in Figure 2.8, where each phase is defined by the novelty of the applications and the complexity of the coordination efforts needed to make them workable.[19]

In view of such an evolution path for blockchain, industry sentiment for the technology in the longer-term is still bullish, with projections that suggest blockchain technology will create more than US$176 billion worth of business value by 2025 and US$3.1 trillion by 2030.[20]

2.2.4.2 *Sector Opportunities and Adoption*

McKinsey undertook a study to analyse the strategic importance of blockchain to major industries (see Figure 2.9).

[19] *"The Truth about Blockchain"*, Harvard Business Review, January–February 2017.

[20] *"Gartner: Blockchain will Deliver $3.1 Trillion Dollars in Value by 2030"*, ConsenSys, June 2019.

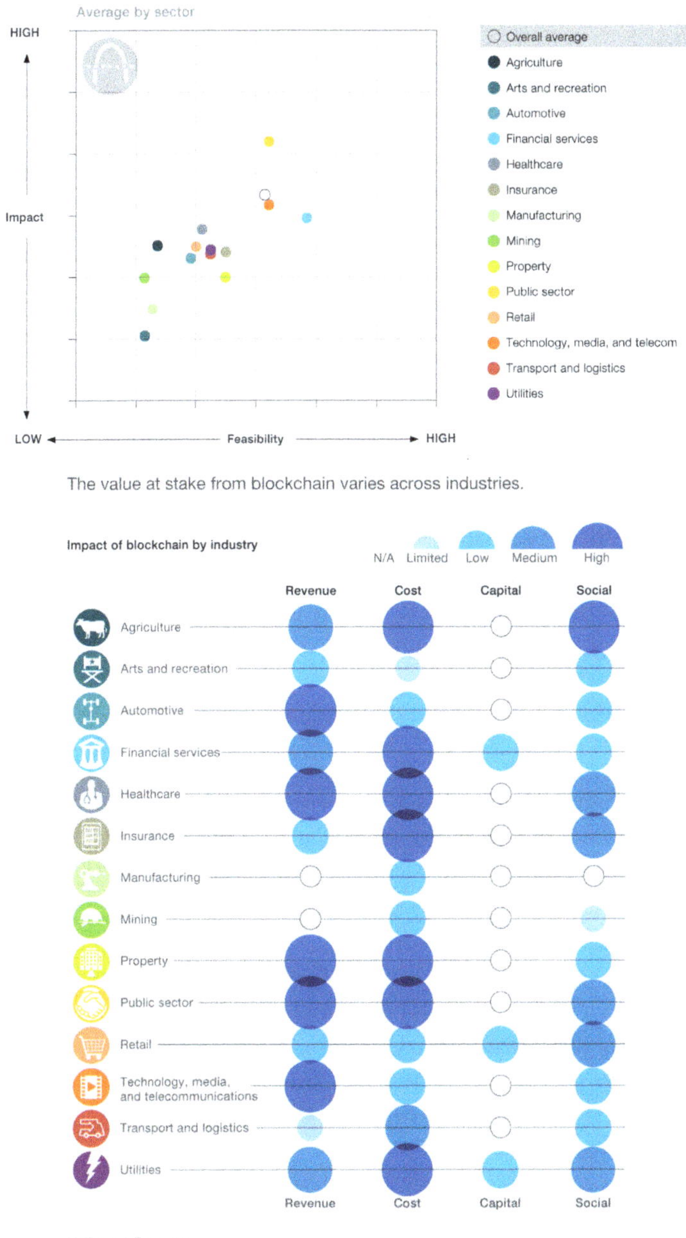

Figure 2.9. Strategic Importance of Blockchain to Major Industries.

Source: *"Blockchain Beyond the Hype — What is the Strategic Business Value?"* McKinsey, June 2018.

The study also indicated that blockchain's short-term value will be predominantly in reducing cost, before creating transformative business models, which is in alignment with the phases of blockchain adoption suggested by *Harvard Business Review* (Figure 2.8). The McKinsey study predicts that blockchain is still three to five years away from feasibility at scale, primarily because of the difficulty of resolving the "coopetition" paradox to establish common standards.

2.2.4.3 *Growth of Public and Private Blockchains*

Table 2.1 illustrates the main types of blockchains, segmented by permission model.

Public permissionless blockchains tend to operate in a less controlled environment, requiring the application of cryptoeconomics to incentivise participants to coordinate. Private permissioned blockchains tend to operate in an environment where participants are already known and vetted, and there are typically off-chain legal contracts and agreements to coordinate participant behaviour.

Table 2.1. Main Types of Blockchains by Permission Model.

			Read	**Write**	**Commit**
Blockchain Types	Open	*Public Permissionless*	Open to anyone	Anyone	Anyone*
		Public Permissioned	Open to anyone	Authorised participants	All or subset of authorised participants
	Closed	*Consortium*	Restricted to an authorised set of participants	Authorised participants	All or subset of authorised participants
		Private Permissioned (Enterprise)	Fully private or restricted to a limited set of authorised nodes	Network operator only	Network operator only

Note: * Requires significant investment either in mining (proof-of-work model) or cryptocurrency itself (proof-of-stake model).

Source: *"Global Blockchain Benchmarking Study"*, Dr Garrick Hileman and Michel Rauchs, 2017.

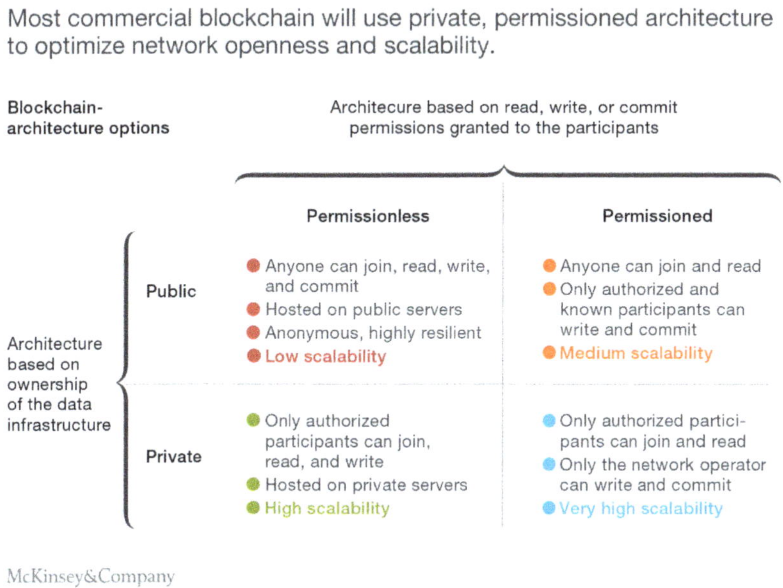

Figure 2.10. Blockchain Architecture Option.

Source: *"Blockchain Beyond the Hype — What is the Strategic Business Value?"* McKinsey, June 2018.

Private permissioned blockchains operate in a more "controlled" environment, and McKinsey suggests that most commercial blockchains will use private, permissioned architecture as presented in Figure 2.10.

This is consistent with research that indicates the private blockchain segment is projected to grow at a higher CAGR. However, whilst private blockchain is currently the leading segment, there is also recognition that the public blockchain segment is expected to experience significant growth.[21] To this end, one of the four transitions projected by Ernst & Young to be driving the progress of blockchain adoption is the transition from private to public networks to create an open system for all users.[22]

---

[21] *"Blockchain Distributed Ledger Market by Type and End User — Global Opportunity Analysis and Industry Forecast, 2017–2023"*, Allied Market Research, March 2017.

[22] *"Regulatory Complexity is the Greatest Barrier to Widespread Blockchain Adoption, While Regulatory Changes are the Primary Driver of Broader Integration"*, EY Poll, June 2018.

The EU Blockchain Observatory and Forum envisions that the first wave of blockchain adoption will be characterised by a large number of permissioned, purpose-built blockchain platforms geared towards a specific use case, and there would be interactions with the off-chain world as well as with each other. In time to come, a global "backbone" of decentralised chains is expected to develop.[23]

2.2.4.4 *Hybrid Blockchains*

Increasingly, companies are also exploring hybrid blockchains, where an individual entity uses a combination of both public and private blockchain to reap the benefits of both approaches. All participants are part of the public blockchain, however, only selected participants are part of the private network.

In a logistics industry use case, for example, large logistics companies can have many partners, subcontractors, and clients. The private part of a hybrid blockchain solution can be used for transactions among the biggest partners — this will be a permissioned setup where parties can view, transact, and make changes based on permissions they are given. However, adding more parties and establishing their trust takes longer than on a public blockchain. The public part of the hybrid blockchain solution could comprise a large list of subcontractors and small partners (e.g. local transport providers) that will be able to make changes on a public network with an easier process of trust establishment.[24]

2.2.5 *Singapore Market Potential of Blockchain*

For Singapore, the blockchain market has the potential to achieve a range of market spending between US$201 million to US$272 million market in 2022 and US$1.9 billion to US$2.6 billion market by 2030 with a CAGR of 32.5% as indicated by Figure 2.11.

---

[23] *"Scalability, Interoperability and Sustainability"*, EU Blockchain Observatory and Forum, March 2019.

[24] *"Hybrid Blockchain"*, Altcoin Magazine, October 2018.

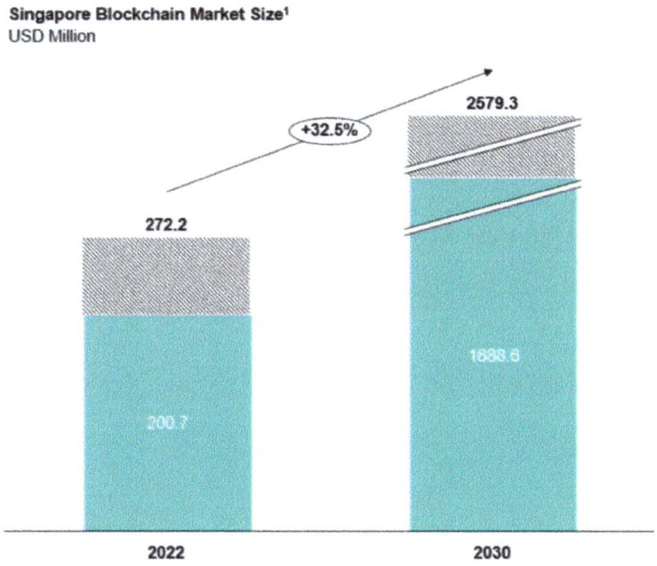

Figure 2.11. Singapore Blockchain Market Size.

Note: [1]Singapore's Blockchain market size is triangulated based on data and insights from: IDC Worldwide Semiannual Blockchain Spending Guide; Gartner Forecast: Enterprise IT Spending by Vertical Industry Market, Worldwide, 2016–2022, 2Q18 Update; Gartner Forecast: Communications Service Provider Operational Technology, Worldwide by Country, 2016–2022; Gartner Broadband Access Systems by Region, 1998–2007; Gartner Consumer Communications Market Revenue 2007–2013; D&B Hoovers.

2.3 Technology Study — AI

2.3.1 *Definition of AI*

AI originated more than 50 years ago, and it is generally agreed that John McCarthy coined the phrase "artificial intelligence" in a written proposal for a workshop in Dartmouth in 1956.[25] AI is now commonly understood as the study and engineering of computations that make it possible to perceive, reason, act, learn, and adapt.[26]

[25] *"The Origins of Artificial Intelligence"*, Rodney Brooks, April 2018.

[26] Presentation by Professor Steven Miller in a corporate AI seminar.

In the widely referenced book, *Artificial Intelligence: A Modern Approach,*[27] Dr Stuart Russell and Dr Peter Norvig define AI as:

> "The study of agents that receive percepts from the environment and perform actions."

The various definitions of AI are laid out along a multi-dimensional framework, i.e.

Thinking humanly;
Thinking rationally;
Acting humanly; and
Acting rationally

"Thinking humanly" and "thinking rationally" are concerned with thought processes and reasoning, whereas "acting humanly" and "acting rationally" address behaviour. "Thinking humanly" and "acting humanly" measure success in terms of fidelity to human performance, whereas "thinking rationally" and "acting rationally" measure against an ideal performance measure, rationality.

2.3.2 *AI Evolution and Branches of AI*

2.3.2.1 *History of AI*

According to many observers, the current AI boom began about seven (7) years ago, following a series of ups and downs, often referred to as "AI summers and winters", as interest in AI has alternately grown and diminished.[28] This is illustrated in Figure 2.12:

---

[27] Adapted from *"Artificial Intelligence: A Modern Approach"*, 3rd edition, 2010, Prentice Hall.

[28] *"WIPO Technology Trends 2019 — Artificial Intelligence"*, World Intellectual Property Organization, 2019.

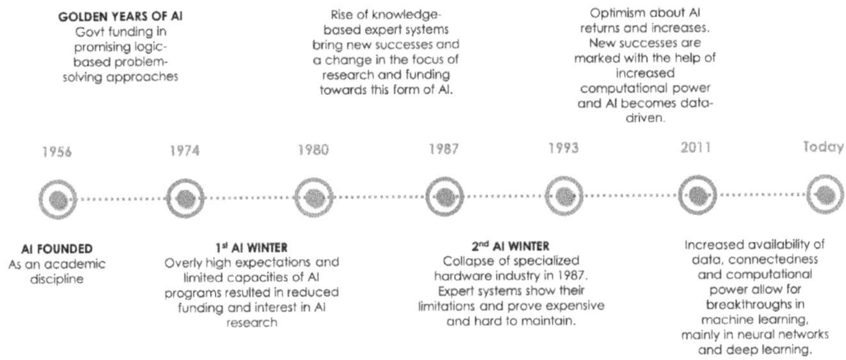

Figure 2.12. AI Summers and Winters.

Source: Information Extracted from *"WIPO Technology Trends 2019 — Artificial Intelligence"*, World Intellectual Property Organization, 2019.

2.3.2.2 *Types of Intelligence*

Most of the current advances in AI have been focused on solving particular kinds of problems or narrowly defined tasks. This is generally referred to as "narrow AI", where the focus is typically on a single subset of cognitive abilities and advances in that spectrum.[29] However, the longer-term goal for many researchers is the creation of "Artificial General Intelligence (AGI)", which refers to the type of adaptable intellect found in humans, a flexible form of intelligence capable of learning how to carry out vastly different tasks. According to Innovation Centre Denmark, the evolution of AI can be categorised into three stages[30] (see Figure 2.13).

A survey conducted among four groups of experts in 2012/2013 by AI researcher Vincent C Muller and philosopher Nick Bostrom reported a 50% chance that AGI would be developed between 2040 and 2050, rising to 90% by 2075.[31]

---

[29] *"What Is Narrow Artificial Intelligence (Narrow AI)? — Definition from Techopedia"*, Technopedia.com.

[30] *"Defining Artificial Intelligence"*, Innovation Centre Denmark, 2018.

[31] *"What Is AI? Everything You Need to Know about Artificial Intelligence"*, ZDNet, February 2018.

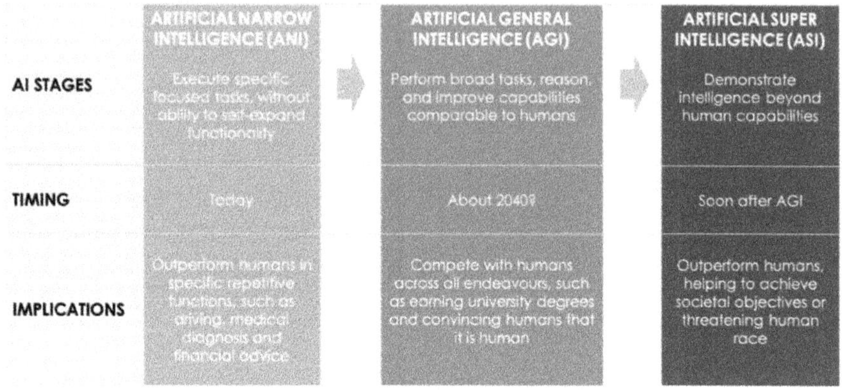

Figure 2.13. Evolution of AI.

2.3.2.3 *Branches of AI*

The field of AI is vast, and comprises different branches. Figure 2.14 summarises the branches and approaches of AI, as discussed in this AI technology roadmap.

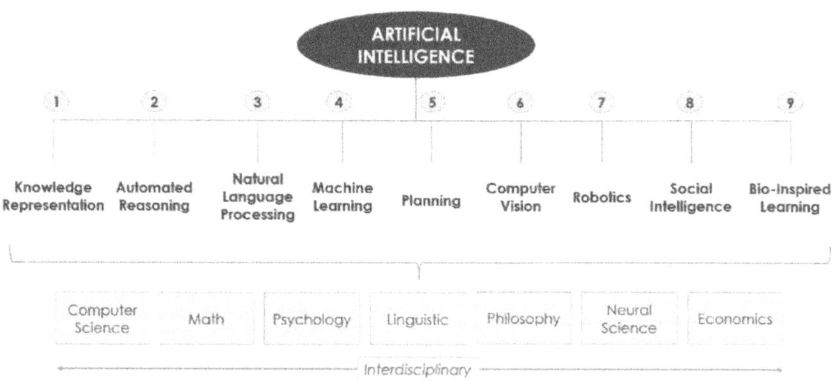

Source: Adaptation of Taiger Presentation Slide at IMDA AI workshop, May 2018

Figure 2.14. Branches of AI.

2.3.2.4 *Use Cases and Applications of AI*

In Figure 2.15, given the number of branches of AI, McKinsey examines a variety of AI and analytics techniques, mapping their applicability to

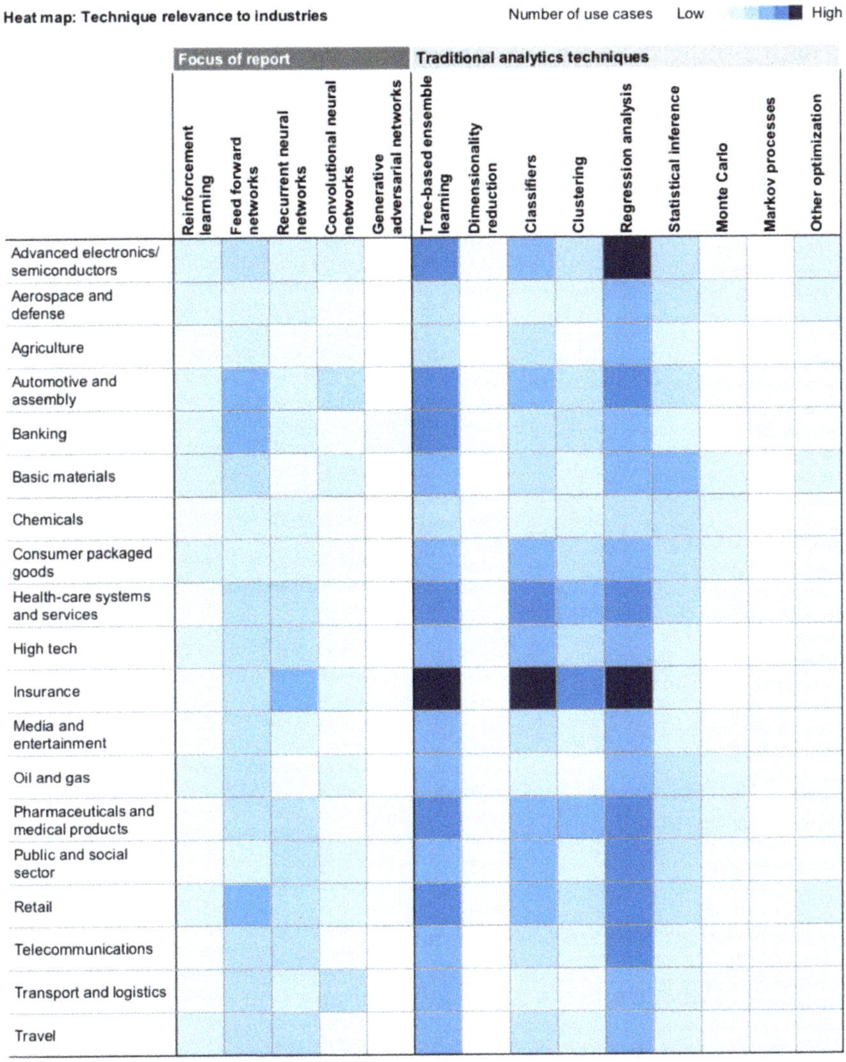

SOURCE: McKinsey Global Institute analysis

Figure 2.15. AI/Analytics Techniques' Relevance to Industries.

industries and functions. It is observed that the applicability of different techniques vary across industries and functions.[32]

---

[32] *"Notes from the AI Frontier: Insights from Hundreds of Use Cases"*, McKinsey, April 2018.

McKinsey suggests that in terms of opportunities, the following industries offer the strongest opportunities for AI globally: public sector, banking, retail, and automotive (see Figure 2.16).

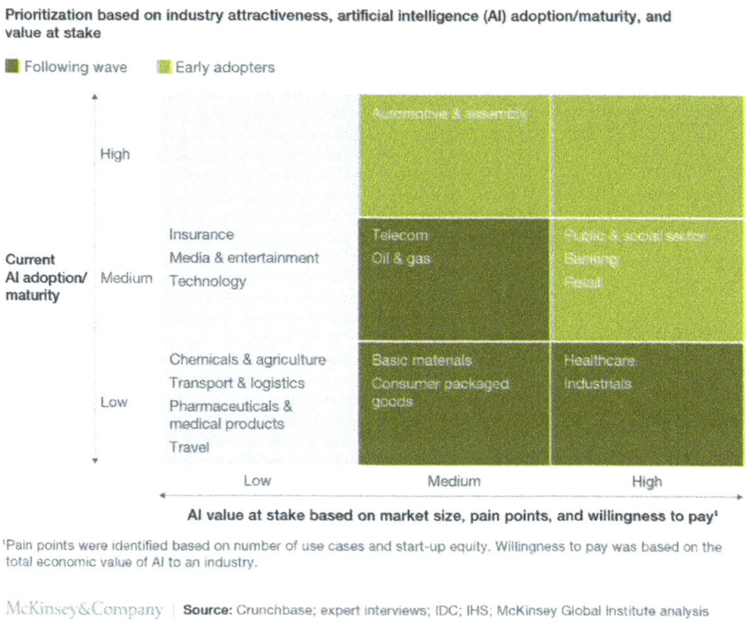

Figure 2.16. Opportunities for AI, by Industry.

Source: *"Artificial Intelligence: The Time to Act is Now"*, McKinsey, January 2018.

2.3.2.5 *Algorithms and Techniques*

2.3.2.5.1 Advancements in AI Innovation

MIT Technology Review analysed 25 years of AI research to understand the evolution of AI research in the past, and how AI would evolve in the future. The analysis uncovered three major trends:

- *Late 1990s and early 2000s — Shift towards machine learning*
  The paradigm of knowledge-based systems declined as researchers realised there were too many rules that needed to be encoded for a system to be intelligent. Words associated with knowledge-based

systems (such as "logic", "constraint", "rule") decreased in frequency (see Figure 2.17). As researchers turned to machine learning to extract rules automatically from data, words associated with machine learning (such as "data", "network", "performance") saw growth.

- *Early 2010s — Rise in popularity of neural networks*
  In the machine learning paradigm, a variety of different methods (such as Bayesian networks, support vector machines, and evolutionary algorithms) were explored before a pivotal breakthrough in deep learning in 2012, and this led to a rise in neural networks.
- *Past few years — Growth in reinforcement learning*
  In the few years since the rise of deep learning, reinforcement learning grew in popularity after the pivotal defeat of the world champion in Go by DeepMind's AlphaGo, which was trained with reinforcement learning.

As every decade sees the reign of different techniques, the 2020s is expected to follow a similar path, which indicates that the era of deep learning could soon come to an end.

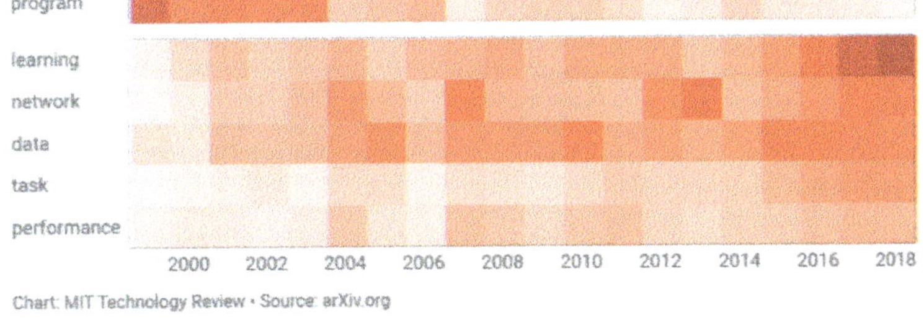

Figure 2.17. Machine Learning Eclipses Knowledge-based Reasoning.

Source: *"We Analyzed 16,625 Papers to Figure Out Where AI is Headed Next"*, MIT Technology Review, January 2019.

2.3.2.5.2 Key AI Breakthroughs

The "State of AI 2019" report outlines the key technological and research breakthroughs[33] from mid-2018 to mid-2019:

- **Reinforcement Learning:** Games have been used as one of the key means to test and evaluate the performance of AI systems. Reinforcement learning saw several notable examples where it surpassed human performance, e.g.
  - OpenAI outperforming humans in Montezuma's revenge[34];
  - DeepMind's StarCraft II program Alpha Star defeated a top professional player[35];
  - DeepMind's demonstration of human-level performance in Quake III Arena Capture the Flag[36]; and
  - OpenAI's Dota 2 defeating 99.4% of players in public matches.[37]

  Anticipated next steps for reinforcement learning include:
  - Play-driven learning for robots[38]: Training a single robot using play to perform many complex tasks without having to re-learn each from scratch;
  - Learning dexterity using simulation and the real world[39];
  - Curiosity-driven explanation[40];
  - Learning dynamic models for online planning[41]; and

---

[33] *"State of AI"*, Nathan Bemaich and Ian Hogarth, June 2019.

[34] *"OpenAI Made a System That's Better at Montezuma's Revenge Than Humans"*, VentureBeat, November 2018.

[35] *"AlphaStar: Mastering the Real-Time Strategy Game StarCraft II"*, DeepMind, January 2019.

[36] *"Capture the Flag: The Emergence of Complex Cooperative Agents"*, DeepMind, May 2019.

[37] *"OpenAI's Dota 2 Bot Defeated 99.4% of Players in Public Matches"*, VentureBeat, April 2019.

[38] *"Learning Latent Plans from Play"*, Google, March 2019.

[39] *"Project Blue"*, UC Berkeley Robot Learning Lab, May 2019.

[40] *"Curiosity and Procrastination in Reinforcement Learning"*, Google, October 2018.

[41] *"Introducing PlaNet: A Deep Planning Network for Reinforcement Learning"*, Google, Februay 2019.

- ○ Moving research into production, e.g. Facebook's release of Horizon, an open-source end-to-end platform that uses applied reinforcement learning to optimise systems in large-scale production environments.[42]

- **Natural Language Processing (NLP):** The advancements in NLP[43] arose from the successful application of transfer learning to NLP. Examples of projects include:
  - ○ Universal Language Model Fine-Tuning (UMLFit) from fast.ai and Sebastian Ruder;
  - ○ Embeddings from Language Models (ELMo) from the Allen's Institute;
  - ○ Transformer from OpenAI; and
  - ○ Bidirectional Encoder Representations from Transformers (BERT) from Google.

  Performance benchmarks such as GLUE and SuperGLUE[44] also enabled performance testing at a variety of language understanding tasks.
- **Federated Learning:** Federated learning was first introduced by Google in 2017. In March 2019, Google released TensorFlow for federated learning, which enables distributed machine learning for developers to train models across many mobile devices without data leaving those devices.
- **Computer Vision[45]:** The release of Generative Adversarial Networks (GANs) in 2014 spawned multiple and diverse applications, however, images generated by machines were still fairly easy to spot. The release of BigGAN[46] represented a step forward for GANs as it resulted in realistic images, making waves in the research community.

---

[42] *"Horizon: The First Open Source Reinforcement Learning Platform for Large-Scale Products and Services"*, Facebook, November 2018.

[43] *"Machine Learning and AI Main Developments in 2018 and Key Trends for 2019"*, KDnuggets, December 2018.

[44] *"Introducing SuperGLUE: A New Hope Against Muppetkind"*, Alex Wang, April 2019.

[45] *"A Technical Overview of AI & ML (NLP, Computer Vision, Reinforcement Learning) in 2018 & Trends for 2019"*, AnalyticsVidhya.com, December 2018.

[46] *"BigGAN: A New State of the Art in Image Synthesis"*, SyncedReview, October 2018.

The technology evolved from generation and replacement of faces (e.g. Synthesia,[47] which offers professional face replacement services by seamlessly changing a presenter or actor's expressions and dialogue) to full-body synthesis (e.g. DataGrid[48] generating fake images of fashion models).

Speech synthesis developed shortly after image and video manipulation, e.g. Dessa's simulation of Joe Rogan's voice.[49]

2.3.2.6 *Hardware*

2.3.2.6.1 Investments in AI Hardware

Much of the spotlight has traditionally been on the developments in AI software, such as new algorithms and techniques (see Table 2.2). However, as AI matures in deployment, it has been driving the development of specialised/optimised hardware to provide the computational abilities and/or architecture to make it possible to run AI algorithms within a reasonable period of time. Whilst AI drives demand for existing chipsets, increasingly, there is also demand for chipsets that are designed or optimised for AI.

McKinsey research suggests that AI-related semiconductors will see growth of about 18% annually over the next few years — five times greater than the rate for semiconductors used in non-AI applications. By 2025, AI-related semiconductors could account for almost 20% of all demand, which would translate into about US$67 billion in revenue (see Figure 2.18).[50]

Most AI chips — both training and inferencing — had previously been developed for data centres. However, as processing shifts towards the edge, the demand for inferencing at the edge is expected to grow. Whilst the market for cloud-based data centre AI chips for training and

---

[47] *"Synthesia: Lip Sync"*, FXGuide, November 2018.

[48] *"Amazing AI Generates Entire Bodies of People Who Don't Exist"*, Futurism, April 2019.

[49] *"This AI-Generated Joe Rogan Voice Sounds Eerily Like the Real Thing"*, Gizmodo, May 2019.

[50] *"Artificial Intelligence Hardware: New Opportunities for Semiconductor Companies"*, McKinsey, January 2019.

Table 2.2. Existing Processors' Support for New AI Applications.

	Strengths	Limitations	Training Rank	Inference Rank
CPU	• General-purpose, in servers and PCs • Sufficient for inference	• Serial-processing is less efficient than parallel processing	N/A	N/A
GPU	• Highly parallel, high-performance • Uses popular AI framework CUDA	• Less efficient than FPGAs • Scalability • Inefficient unless fully utilised	1	3
FPGA	• Reconfigurable • Good for constantly evolving workloads • Efficient	• Difficult to program • Lower performance vs GPUs • No major AI framework	2	2
ASIC	• Best performance • Most energy and cost efficient • Fully customisable	• Long development cycle • Requires high volume to be practical • Quickly outdated, inflexible	3	1

Note: CPU — Central Processing Units; GPU — Graphics Processing Units; FPGA — Field Programmable Gate Arrays; ASIC — Application-Specific Integrated Circuits.
Source: *"AI-Optimised Chipsets — Part I: Key Drivers"*, Vertex Ventures, March 2018.

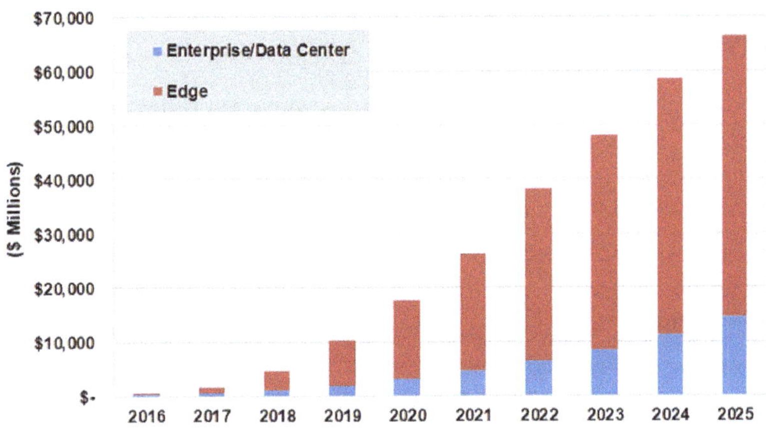

Figure 2.18. Deep Learning Chipset Revenue by Market Sector, World Markets: 2016–2025.

Source: *"NVIDIA's Inference Push for AI"*, Tractica, October 2018.

inferencing is expected to grow, AI chips for inferencing at the edge are expected to grow much more significantly, at 3.5 times[51] larger than the training chipsets in terms of the market potential (see Figure 2.18).

The preferred architectures for compute in data centres and the edge are also expected to evolve (see Figure 2.19).

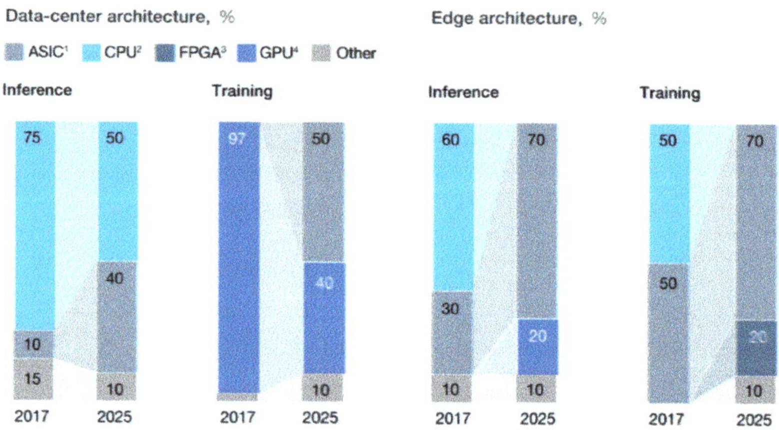

Figure 2.19. Shift in Preferred Architectures for AI Chipsets in the Data Centre and Edge.
Source: *"Artificial Intelligence Hardware: New Opportunities for Semiconductor Companies"*, McKinsey, January 2019.

2.3.2.6.2 Transition in Computing Architecture

New computing architectures, such as neuromorphic and quantum computing, are also developing as well. IBM suggests that the hardware transition from GPUs to the quantum era will happen in three stages[52]:

- **Current–2022:** Utilise GPUs, build new accelerators with conventional CMOS.
- **2022–2026:** Overcoming the von Neumann bottleneck, Analog devices that can combine memory and computation, neuromorphic computing.
- **Beyond 2026:** Quantum computing.

[51] *"NVIDIA's Inference Push for AI"*, Tractica, October 2018.
[52] *"The Future of Hardware is AI"*, IBM, December 2017.

Hardware developments in quantum computing are also triggering new research in quantum AI. For example, researchers from the Centre for Quantum Technologies in Singapore, ETH Zurich, and the University of Oxford published research on a new type of Quantum Machine Learning (QML) algorithm,[53] and there are start-ups looking at using quantum computing to boost machine learning.[54]

2.3.2.7 *Enablement of Deployment of AI*

2.3.2.7.1 AI Frameworks

With the exponential demand for AI, and the growth in the size of the AI community, this has led to the evolution of AI frameworks which make learning AI much easier. Pytorch (open sourced by Facebook), for example, is said to be catching up with TensorFlow,[55] particularly with the adoption of Pytorch in the popular deep learning course fast.ai. Other popular AI frameworks include TensorFlow (created by Google), Caffe/Caffe2, and Microsoft CNTK. Table 2.3 shows a comparison of popular AI frameworks.

An analysis was performed to examine the growth of AI frameworks such as TensorFlow, PyTorch, Keras, and FastAI, with TensorFlow emerging as the most in-demand and fastest-growing framework (see Figure 2.20).

2.3.2.7.2 Drag and Drop, No/Low-Code AI Development Platforms

Beyond AI frameworks, tools and platforms that further simplify AI development for business users are also emerging.

---

[53] *"New Quantum ML Algorithm Could Revolutionise Quantum AI Before It Even Begins"*, 311institute.com, May 2018.
[54] *"A Startup Uses Quantum Computing to Boost Machine Learning"*, MIT Technology Review, December 2017.
[55] *"What were the Most Significant Machine Learning Advances of 2018?"* Forbes, January 2019.

Table 2.3. AI Framework Comparison.

AI framework	Pros	Cons
Pytorch & Torch	• Modularity • Easy to write own later types to be run on GPU • Pre-trained models	• Less plug-and-play • Lack of commercial support • Incomplete documentation
TensorFlow[a]	• Python & Numpy • Computational graph abstraction • TensorBoard for visualisation	• Slower than other frameworks • Not many pre-trained models • Lack of commercial support
Caffe	• Good for feedforward networks and image processing • Good for fine-tuning existing networks • Train models without writing any code	• Need to write C++/CUDA for new GPU layers • Slow development • Lack of commercial support
Caffe2	• More scalable & lightweight compared to Caffe • BSD licence	• Lack of commercial support

Note: [a]TensorFlow 2.0 Alpha Released in March 2019.
Source: *"Comparison of AI Frameworks"*, Skymind.ai.

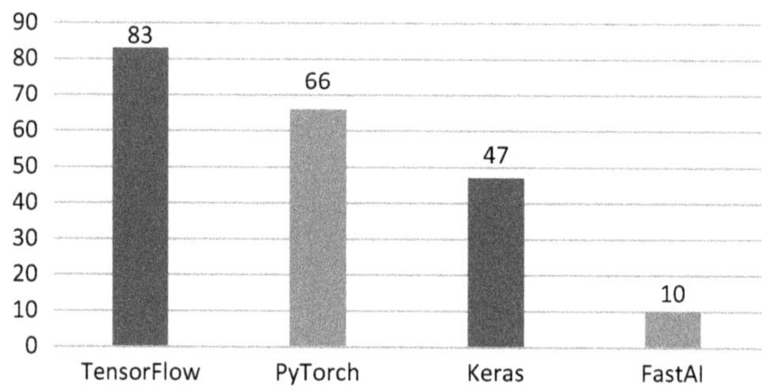

Figure 2.20. Deep Learning Framework Six-Month Growth Scores 2019.
Source: *"Which Deep Learning Framework is Growing Fastest?"* Jeff Hale, April 2019.

Google, for example, launched an alpha release of Cloud AutoML, its first in a set of tools that trains AI without requiring code.[56] Start-ups, such

[56] *"Google Tool Lets You Train AI Without Writing Code"*, Engadget, January 2018.

as Lobe,[57] have also developed AI tools that focus on visual interfaces rather than coding — users use a drag-and-drop interface to build deep learning algorithms.[58] Baidu also created EZDL, which allows users to build personalised machine learning models through a drag-and-drop interface.[59]

2.3.2.8 *Enablement of Trust in AI*

As AI increasingly becomes more pervasive and plays an expanding role in society, there is a need to build trust in AI. To trust computer decisions, there is a need to know how an AI system arrives at its conclusions and recommendations.

Typical causes of learned bias in models[60] include algorithmic bias, e.g. training data is not representative, and human bias, e.g. historical inequity captured in data. Forrester suggests the FAIR framework for ensuring models developed are FAIR,[61] or

- Fundamentally sound;
- Assessable;
- Inclusive;
- Reversible.

2.3.2.8.1 National Efforts in AI Regulation and Governance

In the US, the Commercial Facial Recognition Privacy Act prohibits commercial companies using facial recognition technology from collecting or sharing people's data without their explicit consent. It also would require third-party testing before the technology could be introduced into

---

[57] *"Microsoft Acquires Lobe, a Drag-and-Drop AI Too"*, TechCrunch, September 2018.
[58] *"It's Easier Than You Think to Craft AI Tools Without Typing a Line of Code"*, The Verge, June 2018.
[59] *"Machine Learning without Programming is Now Possible"*, BBVA, December 2018.
[60] *"The Ethics of AI: How to Avoid Harmful Bias and Discrimination"*, Forrester, February 2018.
[61] *"Building Trust in the Age of AI — How Businesses can build Fairness into their Machine Learning Models"*, IBM, July 2018.

the market to ensure it is unbiased and does not harm consumers.[62] This move is supported by key technology companies such as Microsoft and Amazon, in response to facial recognition backlash.[63] The Algorithmic Accountability Act is also being discussed to require companies to assess for algorithmic bias in their systems.[64]

Singapore released Asia's 1st Model AI Governance Framework for broader consultation, adoption and feedback in January 2019[65] and a second edition, which includes additional considerations such as robustness and reproducibility) for greater relevance and usability in January 2020.[66] This Model Framework is the first in Asia to provide detailed and readily implementable guidance to private sector organisations to address key ethical and governance issues when deploying AI solutions, and a copy of the primer is included in Annex A of this publication.

2.3.2.8.2 Explainable AI

On the research front, Defense Advanced Research Projects Agency (DARPA) has been investing in the Explainable AI (XAI) programme[67] to create a suite of machine learning techniques that:

- Produce more explainable models, while maintaining a high level of learning performance; and
- Enable human users to understand, appropriate trust, and effectively manage the emerging generation of artificially intelligent partners.

---

[62] "*New Facial Recognition Bill Would Require Consent Before Companies Could Share Data*", The Verge, March 2019.

[63] "*Amazon Joins Microsoft in Calling for Regulation of Facial Recognition Tech*", Engadget, February 2019.

[64] "*Democrats Draw Up Bill That Would Require Tech Platforms to Assess Algorithmic Bias*", TechCrunch, April 2019.

[65] "*Singapore Releases Asia's First Model AI Governance Framework*", IMDA, January 2019.

[66] "*Singapore and World Economic Forum driving AI Adoption and Innovation*", IMDA, January 2020.

[67] "*Explainable Artificial Intelligence (XAI)*", DARPA.

The Institute for Ethical AI & Machine Learning has also released XAI,[68] an explainability framework for machine learning to facilitate AI developers to introduce explainability and perform bias evaluation in AI systems.

2.3.2.8.3 Algorithmic Audit Tools, Services, and Frameworks

Algorithm audit is a growing area as companies increasingly opt-in to such a process in order to gain their customers' trust.[69] Such demand has also driven the availability of algorithmic audit services (e.g. O'Neil Risk Consulting and Algorithmic Audit started by Cathy O'Neil, author of *Weapons of Mass Destruction*) and tools (e.g. Accenture AI fairness tool[70]). IBM is also proposing a Supplier's Declaration of Conformity to be completed and voluntarily released by AI developers and providers to increase the transparency of their services and to engender trust in them.[71]

2.3.2.9 *Human-Centered AI*

The advancement in AI is progressing rapidly, and increasingly, newer forms of AI can perform tasks associated with both explicit knowledge and tacit human knowledge more accurately than humans.[72] There is increasing focus and attention on human-centered AI design that reflects realistic conception of user needs and human psychology, in order to make AI more effective.

The Human-Centered AI effort at MIT[73] focuses on the design, development, and deployment of AI systems that learn from and collaborate with humans in a deep, meaningful way. Stanford University launched the

---

68 *"XAI — Explainability Framework"*, Institute for Ethical AI and Machine Learning, 2019.

69 *"Want to Prove Your Business is Fair? Audit your Algorithm"*, Wired, May 2018.

70 *"This Tool Lets You See — And Correct — The Bias in an Algorithm"*, FastCompany, June 2018.

71 *"Factsheets for AI Services"*, IBM, August 2018.

72 *"AI Needs Human-Centered Design"*, Wired, 2018.

73 https://hcai.mit.edu.

Institute for Human-Centered Artificial Intelligence[74] in March 2019 to study, guide, and develop human-centered AI technologies and applications.

One example is the rise of the analogue driving experience — research has shown that drivers develop emotional connections to their cars and the driving experience, and the emotive aspect of the driving experience is a key part of car brands.[75] Even as the technology advances, there is a strong need to understand human-centered AI to address the emotive aspects of the product or service consumption.

2.3.2.10 *Technology Roadmap*

Table 2.4 reflects industry's view on the likely evolution and mainstream adoption of AI technology as of publication of the IMDA Services and Digital Economy (SDE) Technology Roadmap in November 2018.

2.4 Technology Study — Blockchain

2.4.1 *Definition of Blockchain*

It is generally agreed that Blockchain first made its public debut in the paper "Bitcoin: A Peer to Peer for Electronic Cash" written by Satoshi Nakamoto in 2008. Blockchain is the underlying technology behind Bitcoin, and since the publication of the paper, it has developed into one of the most significant technologies with the potential to impact many industries.

The blockchain technology space is at the stage of rapid evolution, and whilst these developments are critical in accelerating innovation, there are also differences in industry usage of terminology, resulting in confusion.

The NISTIR 8202 Blockchain Technology Overview document[76] by National Institute of Standards and Technology, US Department of Commerce defines blockchain as:

---

[74] https://hai.stanford.edu.

[75] *"As Cars Become Increasingly Driverless, People are Already Seeking Analogue Motoring Experiences"*, Phys.org, June 2019.

[76] *"NISTIR 8202 Blockchain Technology Overview"*, NIST, October 2018.

> "Blockchains are distributed digital ledgers of cryptographically signed transactions that are grouped into blocks. Each block is cryptographically linked to the previous one (making it tamper-evident) after validation and undergoing a consensus decision. As new blocks are added, older blocks become more difficult to modify (creating tamper resistance). New blocks are replicated across copies of the ledger within the network, and any conflicts are resolved automatically using established rules."

Such a data structure, with the cryptographic linkages between blocks, is visually represented in Figure 2.21.

A blockchain typically has the following components:

- **Cryptography:** Cryptographic techniques such as one-way hash functions are applied. For example, a hash is applied on the entire block to generate a unique identifier for the block. Each block stores the block hash of its predecessor, resulting in a cryptographic linkage of blocks. This architecture makes data stored in the blockchain resistant to tampering.
- **P2P network:** Network for peer discovery and data sharing in a peer-to-peer fashion.
- **Consensus mechanism:** In the absence of a central coordinating party, an algorithm is needed to determine the ordering of transactions in an adversarial environment (i.e. assuming not every participating node is honest).
- **Ledger:** List of transactions bundled together in cryptographically linked "blocks".
- **Validity rules:** Common set of rules of the network (i.e. what transactions are considered valid, how the ledger gets updated, etc.).

2.4.2 *Key Differences Between Blockchain and Distributed Ledger Technology*

The terminology around blockchain technology can be confusing, and there is a lack of agreement in the community as to whether a blockchain is the same as a distributed ledger technology.

Table 2.4. Likely Evolution and Mainstream Adoption of AI Technology.

	Now–2 Years	**3–5 Years**	**> 5 Years**
General trends			
General	• Narrow AI in selected verticals	• Narrow AI in more verticals	• Broad, human-like AI
Algorithms & techniques			
Knowledge representation	• Knowledge representation for specific domains, e.g. search applications	• Graph analytics • Knowledge graphs	• Ontology learning
Automated reasoning	• Predictive analytics • Automated reasoning for specific domains[a]	• Integration of sensor networks, signal processing, and machine learning to support decision-making for applications	• Prescriptive analytics • General automated reasoning
Natural language processing	• Natural language Q&A in specific domains,[b] e.g. enterprise chat bots • Speech-to-speech translation in specific domains, e.g. lifestyle devices such as Google Home, Amazon Alexa • Image captioning in specific domains[c] • Natural sounding text to speech[d] • Summarisation in specific domains, e.g. computer-generated news stories	• Text-to-Text general translation, e.g. over various context and languages, e.g. Google Translate • Speech recognition for specific domains[e] • Natural language generation	• Combination of natural language processing and computer vision, e.g. visual question answering[f] • Natural language interaction[g] • Advanced speech recognition, e.g. mixed languages, overlapping speeches, noisy environment • Summary generation from multiple sources[h]

Machine learning	• Predictive analytics • Ensemble learning[i] • Deep learning for specific applications, e.g. game-playing (AlphaGo), computer vision (CNNs), speech recognition & synthesis (LSTM models) • Reinforcement learning for specific applications, e.g. computing gaming	• Transfer learning in specific domains, e.g. learning from training in simulation could be applied to physical robots	• Prescriptive analytics • Generative Adversarial Networks (GANs) for specific applications • Lean and augmented data learning • One-shot or zero shot learning • Robust deep learning, e.g. capsule networks • Extreme learning machines • Training AI systems to develop other AI systems, e.g. automated machine learning and deep learning[j]
Planning	• Dynamic and real-time planning, scheduling, and optimisation, e.g. in-vehicle routing and optimising goods delivery, with real-time data input of traffic conditions		
Computer vision	• Real-time gesture recognition for specific applications • Facial and object recognition	• Real-time multi-object and relation detection • Image recognition on extremely large images	• Activity recognition — Understanding the context of the environment as the same actions in different context may have different meanings
Robotics	• Robotic systems for systematic & mundane tasks, e.g. robots in warehouses, autonomous delivery drones	• Assistive robots capable of basic interactions with humans,[k] e.g. robots for customer service in banks and retail, delivery robots in hotels and hospitals	• Hybrid teams of autonomous agents (different vendors & software) acting in collaboration across large geographic areas

(Continued)

Table 2.4. *(Continued)*

	Now–2 Years	3–5 Years	> 5 Years
Social intelligence	• Limited social intelligence, e.g. inference of human emotion through face analysis[l]	• Enhanced social intelligence, e.g. inference of human emotion through multi-modal inputs[m]	• Simulation of human traits, e.g. human emotional intelligence[n]
Bio-inspired learning		• Swarm intelligence and evolutionary computational techniques[o] for specific applications, e.g. scheduling	
Enablement of AI deployment			
AI frameworks	• Enhancements of AI frameworks for CPU, GPU, and/or low-power environment[p]	• Adaptation of AI frameworks for FPGA[q]	
AI Enablement software	• AI developer toolkits[r]	• Abstracted, higher-level AI toolkits and software[s] for less experienced developers and/or tech-savvy business users • Training AI systems to develop other AI systems, e.g. automated machine learning and deep learning	• Highly abstracted, AI-assisted AI toolkits for business users[t]
Enablement of trust in AI			
AI governance	• Organisation-level frameworks & guidelines[u]	• Common and standardised industry frameworks & guidelines[v]	
Explainable AI		• AI algorithms that support explainability through examples, attention heat maps	• AI algorithms that support explainability through discriminative models, deep neural networks dissection

Software tools and services	• Tests and tools[w] assessing fairness and/or bias in data input, algorithms, etc	• Algorithmic audit services[x]	
AI hardware[y]			
CPU	• AI-optimised CPU[z]		
GPU	• AI-optimised GPU[i] • Energy-efficient, low-power GPU accelerators		• Multi-chip module design for GPU accelerators
FPGA		• AI-optimised FPGAs[ii] • Energy-efficient, lower-power FPGA for edge computing applications	• Heterogeneous, adaptive and fast FPGA platform[iii]
ASIC		• AI-optimised ASICs	
Neuromorphic computing			• Neuromorphic-optimised AI
Quantum computing			• Quantum-optimised AI[iv]

Note: [a]Reasoning on data and providing analysis to complement human professionals in decision-making process in specific domains and use cases, e.g. medical diagnosis and prediction.

[b]Systems that automatically answer questions posed by humans in a natural language, and are generally trained using domain-specific data.

[c]Uses a combination of computer vision and natural language processing technologies to provide a short description of what is in an image.

[d]Aims to mimic and replicate human voice, and reproduce audio words that may not have been spoken by human subjects.

[e]Speech recognition engines generally work well with clear speech, quiet environment, and when trained using targeted application corpus.

[f]AI systems that allow questions to be posed in a natural language about images or a video sequence.

[g]The ability to converse on both general and specific topics with an AI agent.

[h]Automatically summarise various related articles or documents in a coherent manner without repeating the points and paraphrasing the articles or documents.

[i]Use of multiple learning algorithms to obtain better predictive performance compared to the use of any of the constituent learning algorithms alone.

[j]Examples — Google Cloud AutoML uses several machine learning techniques to automatically build and train a deep-learning algorithm.

[k]This would require robotic systems to sense and process sensory information (machine perception), perform basic interactions with humans, and assist in simple tasks to improve human productivity.

[l]Examples — Microsoft Face API, deepai.org.

(*Continued*)

Table 2.4. *(Continued)*

[m]Examples — Multi-modal emotion AI.

[n]*"3 Ways AI is Getting More Emotional"*, Harvard Business Review, July 2018.

[o]Evolutionary computation refers to a set of techniques that is inspired by the natural evolution processes — The algorithms generally consist of principles such as mutation, crossover, reproduction, cloning, survival of the fittest, and are population-based methods.

[p]Examples — TensorFlow roadmap for TensorFlow 2.0 indicates support for distributed environment (multiple GPUs and TPU cores), GPU optimisation, TensorFlow Lite for low-power environments.

[q]Examples — Adapting TensorFlow for FPGA, FPGA acceleration of Convolutional Neural Networks (CNNS), Intel OpenVINO toolkit with FPGA support.

[r]Examples — TensorFlow, Microsoft CNTK, Caffe, Theano, Amazon Machine Learning, Torch, Accord.Net, Apache Mahout, Spark MLib.

[s]Example — Google Auto ML for developers with limited machine learning expertise, Lobe drag-and-drop GUI for building deep learning algorithms (*Note*: Acquired by Microsoft in September 2018).

[t]Example — Drag-and-drop, GUI-driven, AI-assisted design tool for AI algorithms.

[u]Example — Google disclosing ethical framework on the use of AI.

[v]Examples of initiatives that have already started include Partnership on AI, Singapore Government Advisory Council on the Ethical use of AI and Data.

[w]Examples — IBM cloud tool to detect AI bias and explain automated decisions, Microsoft tool to detect AI bias, Accenture Fairness Tool.

[x]Example — O'Neil Risk Consulting and Algorithmic Audit.

[y]*"Hitting the Accelerator: The Next Generation of Machine-Learning Chips"*, Deloitte, 2017.

[z]Example — Intel's Knights Mill chip is said to offer machine learning performance 4x superior to that of data centre CPUs not optimised for machine learning.

[i]Example — Nvidia's Volta architecture is said to be 12x better at deep learning training and 6x better at inference than the preceding Pascal architecture.

[ii]Example — Google Tensor Processing Unit (TPU), Intel Nervana chip, Fujitsu Deep Learning Unit (DLU).

[iii]Example — Xilinx Adaptive Compute Acceleration Platform (ACAP), which is both hardware and software programmable, and can dynamically adapt to various workloads and applications.

[iv]Example — Quantum machine learning.

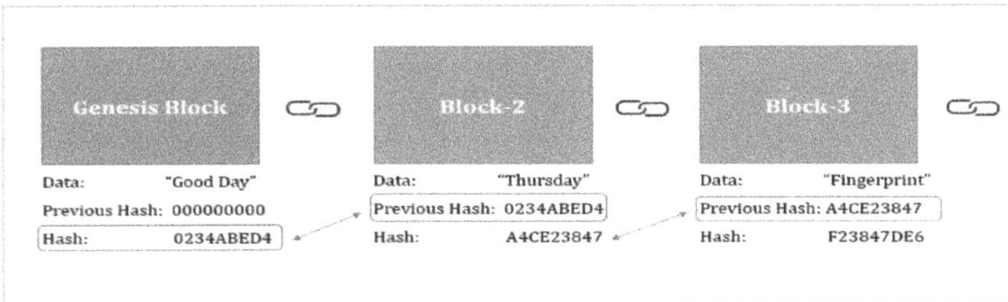

Figure 2.21. Blocks in a Blockchain.

Source: *"Blockchain Key Characteristics and the Conditions to Use It as a Solution"*, Venkat Kasthala, August 2018.

The first blockchains that emerged were closely based on the architecture of Bitcoin, where blocks are used as data structures. Subsequently, new database systems that emerged are also often referred to as blockchains, but may not share the main characteristics of "traditional" blockchains, e.g. some are "block-less", others do not broadcast all transactions to each participant, etc. The more generic phrase "distributed ledger technology" emerged as an umbrella term to describe these technologies, but in practice in industry, "blockchain" and "distributed ledger technology" is often used interchangeably.

In the context of this publication, the broader umbrella of distributed ledger technologies are considered, despite the use of the shorter terminology "blockchain".

Figure 2.22 illustrates the differences between distributed databases, distributed ledgers, and blockchains.

- **Distributed databases:** Do not have a central "master" database, and are replicated across multiple nodes and devices that collaborate to maintain a consistent view of the database state;
- **Distributed ledgers:** The design is premised on an adversarial threat model that mitigates the presence of malicious nodes in the network, and are designed to be Byzantine fault-tolerant; and
- **Blockchains:** A subset of distributed ledgers that use a data structure that bundles transactions into blocks, and/or the broadcast of data to all participants.

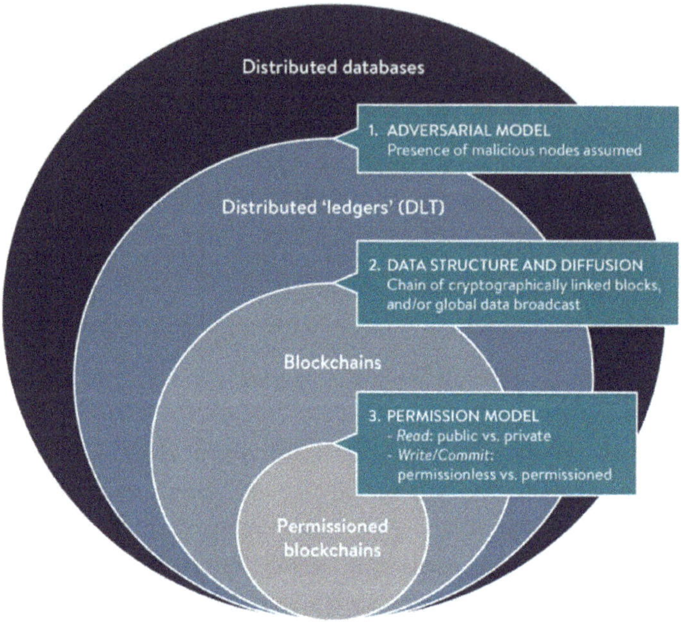

Figure 2.22. Blockchain, Distributed Ledger, and Distributed Database.
Source: *"Global Blockchain Benchmarking Study"*, Dr Garrick Hileman & Michel Rauchs, 2017.

2.4.3 *Public and Enterprise Blockchains*

Table 2.1 illustrates the main types of blockchains by permission models.

Public permissionless blockchains tend to operate in a less controlled environment, requiring the application of cryptoeconomics to incentivise participants to coordinate. Bitcoin and Ethereum are examples of public permissionless blockchain networks.

Private permissioned blockchains tend to operate in an environment where participants are already known and vetted, and there are typically off-chain legal contracts and agreements to coordinate participant behaviour. As an example, Quorum is a private blockchain powered using the Ethereum network.

An emerging development is the hybrid blockchain, which is the combination of both public and private blockchains to reap the benefits of both approaches. The hybrid blockchain consists of the public blockchain (that all participants are a part of) and a private network that restricts participation to those invited by a centralised body. XinFin is an example of a hybrid blockchain, using Ethereum for the public component and Quorum for the private component of their solution.

2.4.4 *Key/Emerging Developments in Blockchain*

The subsequent sections of this chapter examine key/emerging developments in blockchain in the following:

- Applications of blockchain;
- Decentralised architecture;
- Network;
- Security & privacy;
- Smart contracts;
- Blockchain interoperability;
- Post-quantum blockchain; and
- Standards development.

2.4.4.1 *Applications of Blockchain*

2.4.4.1.1 Evolution of Blockchain Technology

Since the publication of the Bitcoin paper in 2009, introducing blockchain technology to the world, the application of blockchain has evolved and diversified (see Figure 2.23). The first generation of blockchain in the 2010s revolved around Bitcoin and cryptocurrencies. With the development of Ethereum and smart contracts, the application of blockchain extended beyond the finance sector, and has since gained recognition for its potential to transform various industries.[77] However, technology challenges, such as performance and scalability, interoperability and privacy remain, and the third generation of blockchain is under development.[78]

---

[77] *"Banking is Only the Beginning: 58 Big Industries Blockchain Could Transform"*, CBInsights, April 2020.

[78] *"Blockchain Generations"*, MeetNoor.com, November 2018.

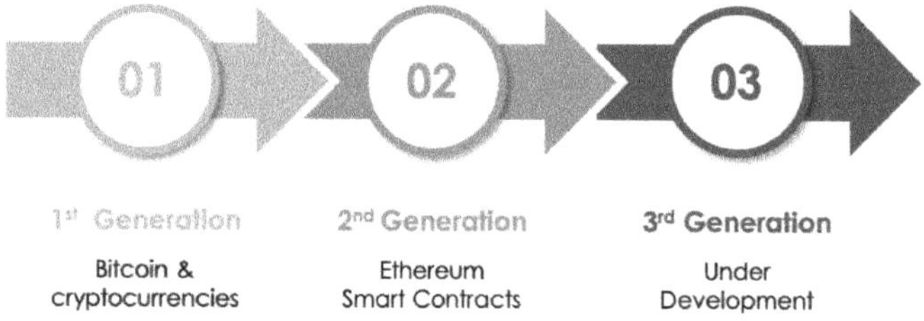

Figure 2.23. Blockchain Generations.

Figure 2.24 examines the timeline of blockchain developments, projecting that the next few years will focus on addressing the technology challenges to bring blockchain to its third generation.

2.4.4.1.2 Key Features of Blockchain

Blockchain is associated with the following key features[79] as in Figure 2.25:

- **Immutability of record:** The cryptographic linkages between blocks in the blockchain make data stored in the blockchain tamper-resistant. Once a transaction is written into the blockchain, it cannot be deleted. Should an error be made, another transaction can be written, however, the trail of transactions is preserved. This feature imparts confidence in the provenance of the value being transacted and enhances fraud detection.
- **Disintermediation of trust:** There is no central party in the network, mitigating against third party risk. Instead, trust is distributed over the network, rather than centralised.
- **Smart contracts:** These are self-executing commitments. Obligations codified by smart contracts are easily replicable, and enjoy the benefit of security, verifiability, transparency, and immutability of the blockchain.

These features have seen the growth of blockchain being applied in various use cases and industries.

[79] *"Blockchain 2.0"*, Credit Suisse, January 2018.

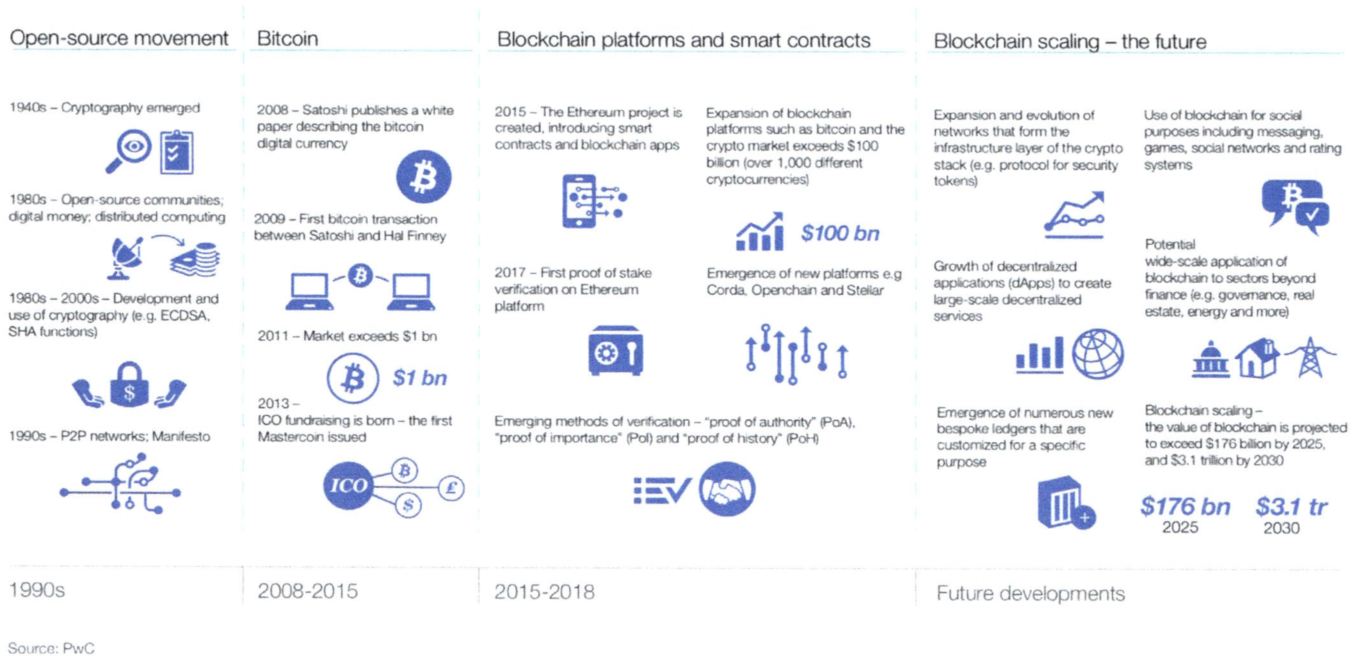

Figure 2.24. Timeline of Blockchain Developments.

Source: *"Building Blockchains for a Better Planet"*, World Economic Forum, September 2018.

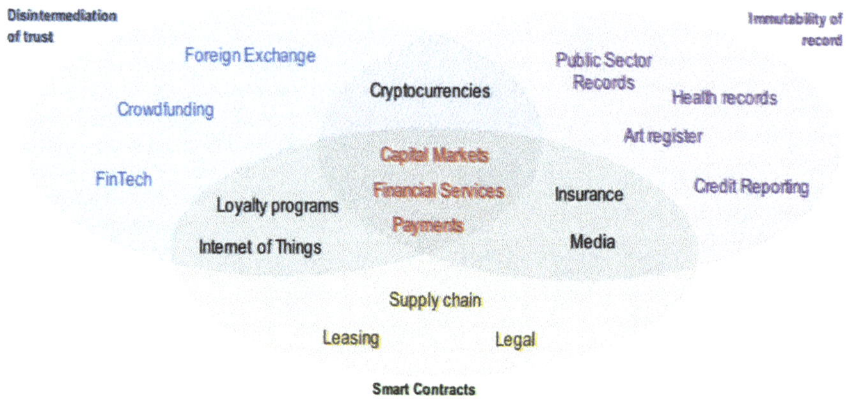

Figure 2.25. Three Disruptive Benefits of Blockchain and Potential Applications.
Source: *"Blockchain 2.0"*, Credit Suisse, January 2018.

2.4.4.2 *Decentralised Architecture*

2.4.4.2.1 Taxonomy

Blockchain technology is under active development, the terminology is evolving and formal definitions are in the process of being established. The lack of clarity about, and inconsistent understanding of the terminology used is one of the challenges encountered. A report[80] on the prospects of standards in blockchain suggests that using standards to establish a stronger consensus on consistent terminology and vocabulary could improve understanding of the technology and help progress the market.

Figure 2.26 shows one example illustrating the representation of the blockchain technology stack.

2.4.4.2.2 Decentralisation

Vitalik Buterin, the co-founder of Ethereum, describes three dimensions of decentralisation[81]:

---

[80] *"Distributed Ledger Technologies/Blockchain: Challenges, Opportunities, and the Prospects for Standards"*, British Standards Institution (NSI) and RAND Europe, May 2017.

[81] *"The Meaning of Decentralisation"*, Vitalik Buterin, September 2017.

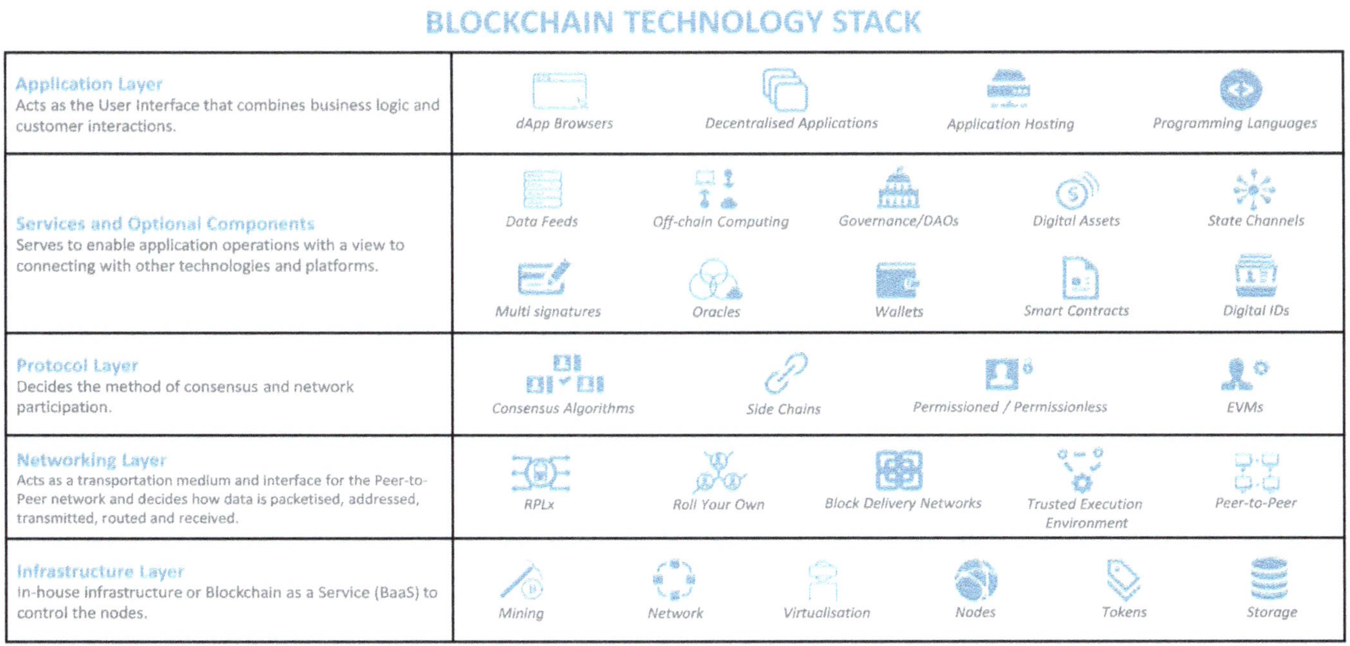

Figure 2.26. Blockchain Technology Stack.

Source: Adapted from *"Blockchain Technology Stack"*, Reddit, 2018.

- **Architectural decentralisation:** The number/diversity of physical computers a system comprises;
- **Political decentralisation:** The number/diversity of individuals or organisations that control the computers that the system is made of; and
- **Logical decentralisation:** The interfaces and data structures that the system presents and maintains (i.e. amorphous swarm as opposed to monolithic).

2.4.4.2.3 Governance

There are different dimensions to blockchain governance, and Figure 2.27 outlines the various dimensions discussed in the industry.

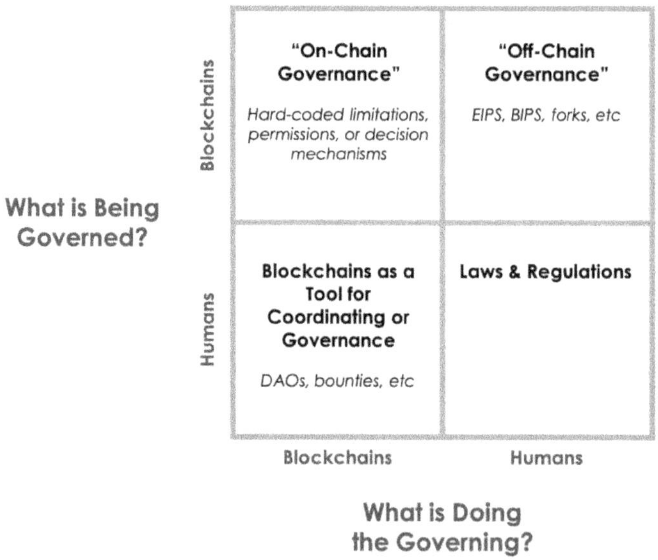

Figure 2.27. Dimensions of Blockchain Governance.

Source: *"Blockchain Communities and Their Emergent Governance"*, Steven McKie, November 2018.

This publication will examine blockchain governance along the dimensions of the governance of blockchains, either by humans (off-chain governance) or blockchains (on-chain governance).

Due to the lack of architectural and political centralisation in blockchain governance, i.e. coming to a consensus on decisions amongst decentralised nodes, is one of the most important aspects of blockchain design. The primary function of blockchain governance is said to act as a self-sustaining mechanism to allow for maximum improvement and growth for all participants (subjective) in the ecosystem.[82]

In a blockchain, the critical components of governance include (i) the incentives, and (ii) the mechanisms for coordination, where a major factor considers the extent of coordination on-chain vs off-chain.[83]

The early blockchain projects are characterised by unspecified governance mechanisms. In subsequent generations, the trend leaned towards off-chain, specific governance structures to handle disagreements.[84] The past few years saw several examples of controversial governance decisions in second-generation blockchains (e.g. Decentralised Autonomous Organisation (DAO) Hack in May/June 2016, Bitcoin scaling debate in August 2017), which probably triggered new developments such as Tezos, Dfinity, and Polkadot, which leaned towards on-chain governance.[85]

This evolution of blockchain governance is illustrated in Table 2.5. As mentioned previously, these are some examples of controversial governance decisions blockchains with off-chain governance.

2.4.4.2.4 Decentralised Autonomous Organisation Hack in May/June 2016[86]

The DAO was a form of investor-directed venture capital fund instantiated on Ethereum blockchain; the DAO is stateless, with unclear rules on how to regulate the DAO (decentralised fund with no centralised management

---

[82] *"Blockchain Governance: How Decentralised do We Need to Be?"* Stephen Laird, April 2018.

[83] *"Blockchain Governance: Programming Our Future"*, Fred Ehrsam, November 2017.

[84] *"Revisiting the On-Chain Governance vs Off-Chain Governance Discussion"*, Pool of Stake, May 2018.

[85] *Ibid.*

[86] *"A Short History of Blockchain Governance or How to Deal with Unexpected Conflict"*, Pool of Stake, May 2018.

Table 2.5. Evolution in Blockchain Governance Design.

	Unspecified blockchain governance	**Off-chain blockchain governance**	**On-chain blockchain governance**
Decision-making	• Unspecified mechanisms	• Involves social coordination • Is afterwards encoded into the protocol by the developers	• Governance rules are hardcoded into the blockchain protocol
Examples		*Bitcoin* *Incentives*: For developers, miners, users *Mechanisms for coordination*: Off-chain — Bitcoin developers share improvement proposals (BIPs) through mailing list	*Tezos* • Any Tezos developer can submit a change to governance structure through code update — Broadcast improvement proposal on-chain • On-chain voting → Implement on testnet • Final vote → Implement on mainnet
		Ethereum *Incentives*: Similar to Bitcoin *Mechanisms for coordination*: Off-chain — Ethereum collects improvement proposals (EIPs) on GitHub	*Dfinity* • Allow on-chain votes to the rules of the system and direct, retroactive change to the ledger
"Roll back" Undesirable Past Actions		Through system forks[a]	Through votes to "undo" the action

Note: [a]As defined by NIST, system forks refer to changes to a blockchain network's protocol and data structures.
Source: *"Revisiting the On-Chain Governance vs Off-Chain Governance Discussion"*, Pool of Stake, May 2018.

structure). The DAO was attacked and a third of the Ether committed to the DAO was stolen. There was a mixed response in the community as to how to deal with the situation — one school of thought was along the lines of "code is law" — that although the hackers' behaviour was unethical, what the code allows is valid and the withdrawal of funds from the DAO was valid. Others demanded that the stolen Ether be returned to the owners. Ethereum eventually hard forked to refund the stolen Ether.

2.4.4.2.5 Bitcoin Scaling Debate in August 2017[87]

Some in the community suggest an increase in block size to counter slow transactions in the network — When the rate of transactions exceeds the available space in the blocks, transactions have to be backlogged, which means that in total transaction rate has to slow down. Bitcoin subsequently forked into Bitcoin Cash, which increased the block size from 1 MB as in Bitcoin classic to up to 32 MB. The increase in block size is seen as controversial because in the eyes of some community members it encourages centralisation.

Other emerging governance strategies[88] include:

- Futarchy, described as the governance technique of evaluating policies ex post while relying on a prediction market to determine the best policy ex ante[89] (e.g. Amoveo, Tezos, Ethereum Gnosis[90]);
- Liquid democracy (e.g. a movement led by David Ernst in San Francisco,[91] Democracy Earth Foundation's governance platform[92]); and
- Quadratic voting, where participants can purchase extra votes to have a greater say in certain issues.

---

[87] *Ibid.*

[88] *"Blockchain Governance: Programming Our Future"*, Fred Ersham, November 2017.

[89] *"Towards Futarchy in Tezos"*, Arthur Breitman, August 2018.

[90] *"On Governance: Futarchy"*, Rocco, January 2019.

[91] *"Liquid Democracy Uses Blockchain to Fix Politics, and Now You can Vote for It"*, TechCrunch, February 2018.

[92] *"Liquid Democracy: Blockchains and Governance in the Post Nation-State Era"*, GovFresh, January 2019.

2.4.4.2.6 Emerging Multi-Disciplinary Areas

The issues discussed above exemplify the multi-disciplinary foundation of blockchain, and Figure 2.28 shows the intersection of multiple fields:

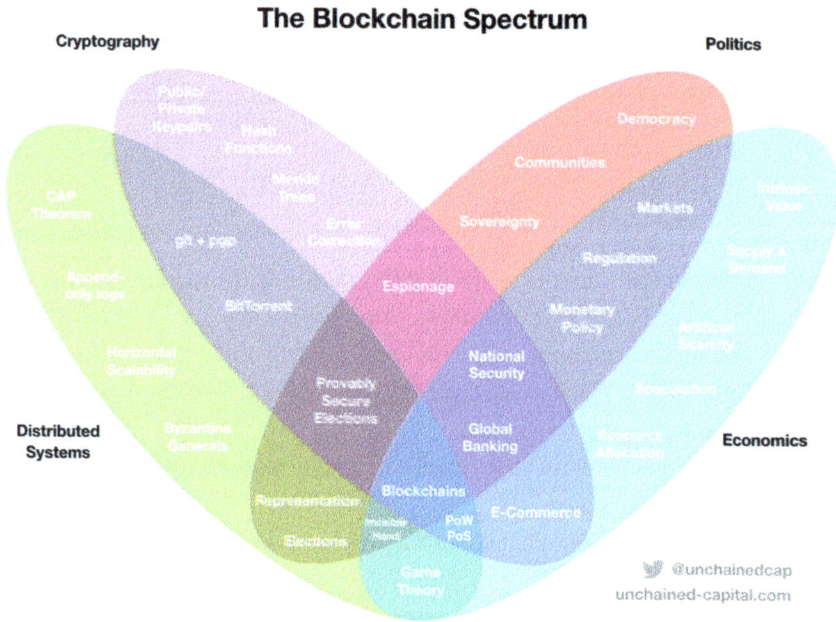

Figure 2.28. Blockchain Spectrum.

Source: *"Why It's Hard to "Get" Bitcoin: The Blockchain Spectrum"*, Unchained Capital, December 2017.

2.4.4.3 *Network*

In a decentralised blockchain network, in the absence of a central party, consensus mechanisms are used to reach agreement in the network. In public blockchains such as Bitcoin and Ethereum, the Proof-of-Work consensus mechanism is commonly used. It provides the economic incentives for miners not to cheat, it provides the needed security, however, it is challenging to scale (e.g. throughput) as the size of the network increases, and it is also very energy-consuming (see Figure 2.29).

As such, there are significant developments ongoing to explore alternative solutions for public blockchains to scale up, so that it can open

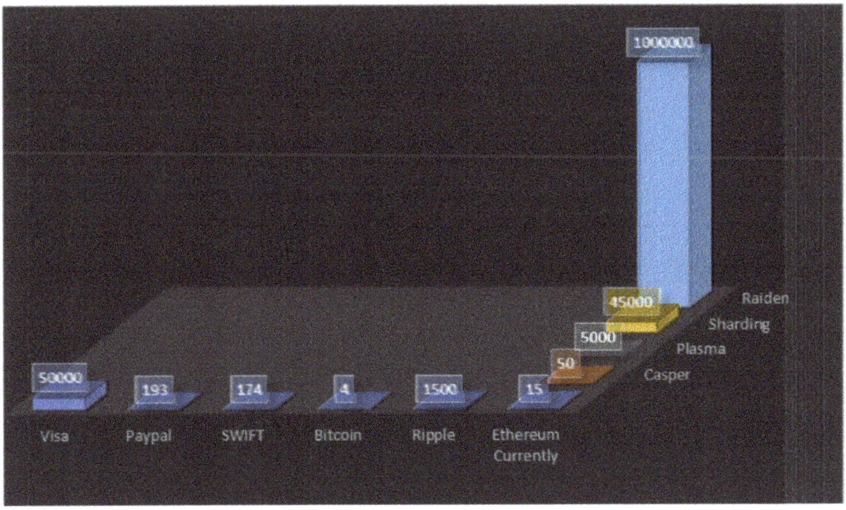

Figure 2.29. Throughput of Blockchains and "Incumbents".

Source: *"How do Casper, Plasma and Other Ethereum Upgrades Works?"* Dean Schmid, February 2018.

up opportunities for blockchain adoption and deployment in high-throughput applications. Ethereum's co-founder, Vitalik Buterin, has articulated the need for Ethereum to process 100,000 transactions per second (over its current 15 transactions per second) for it to be a viable platform in the future.[93]

These various blockchain scalability efforts are summarised in Figure 2.30.

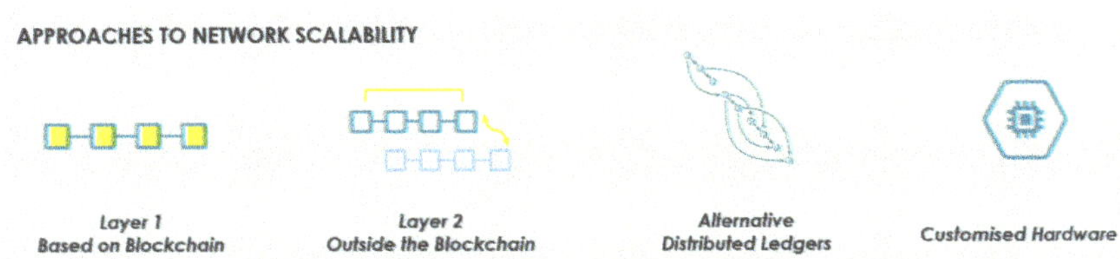

Figure 2.30. Approaches to Network Scalability.

93 *"Vitalik on Ethereum: "Right Now it Can Process 15 Transactions Per Second. Really, We Need 100,000""*, InvestInBlockchain, March 2019.

2.4.4.3.1 Layer 1

Layer 1 approaches refer to development efforts being explored within the blockchain to improve scalability.

- ***Data Structures*****:** Specific to Bitcoin scalability, there are ongoing efforts on modifying the Bitcoin data structures to improve scalability. Segregated Witness (SegWit) is an update to Bitcoin to increase the block size limit from 1 MB (1,000,000 bytes) to a 4,000,000 "weight" limit, and allows the implementation of "layer 2" solutions for further improvement.[94] SegWit was integrated into the Bitcoin network in August 2017 and has reached 40% adoption in May 2018.[95] SegWit2x was proposed to increase the block size from 1 MB to 2 MB and was planned to be a hard fork to be activated three months after Segwit, however, this was subsequently cancelled due to a lack of consensus. Section 2.4.4.2.5 briefly describes the Bitcoin scaling debates.
- ***Consensus*****:** There are also ongoing efforts to evolve the consensus mechanisms to achieve network scalability. For example, Ethereum is expected to transition to the Proof-of-Stake consensus mechanism in 2019,[96] and the Constantinople hard fork as a preliminary step to pave the shift from Proof-of-Work to Proof-of-Stake was completed in February 2019.[97] However, there are roadblocks in the journey towards Proof-of-Stake, e.g. the interest to ensure Ethereum remains decentralised, whilst also ensuring a low barrier of entry for network validators.[98]
- ***Sharding*****:** In databases, sharding is a method for horizontally partitioning data i.e. breaking up the database into "shards" that, when

[94] *"Understanding SegWit and the Bitcoin Scaling Debate"*, Brendan McManus, September 2017.

[95] *"Segwit Transactions Reach Historical Peaks"*, Ethereum World News, May 2018.

[96] *"Ethereum Sharding Slated for 2020: ETH Foundation Researcher Justin Drake"*, CCN, July 2018.

[97] *"Ethereum Constantinople, St Petersburg Upgrades Have Been Activated"*, CoinTelegraph, February 2019.

[98] *"4 Things that Concern Vitalik Buterin about Moving Ethereum to Proof-of-Stake"*, TheNextWeb, March 2019.

aggregated together, form the original database. When sharding is applied in the context of blockchains, instead of the full node storing the entire state of the blockchain, nodes are grouped into subsets, and they process transactions specific to that shard, so that the system can process many transactions in parallel, hence improving throughout.[99] Ethereum is expected to implement sharding over two phases, in 2020 and 2021, respectively.[100] Ethereum is not the only blockchain using sharding for scalability — its implementation is that of state sharding. Other blockchains, such as Ziliqa, focus on network and transaction sharding, and it launched its sharding mainnet in January 2019.[101]

2.4.4.3.2 Layer 2

Layer 2 approaches refer to development efforts being explored outside of the blockchain to improve scalability, and the key efforts are as follows:

- State channels; and
- Side chains.

State channels improve scalability by moving state-altering operations off the chain to achieve improvements in cost and speed, whilst sidechains are separate blockchains that are attached to their parent blockchain (mainchain).

Figure 2.31 illustrates the conceptual differences between state channels and side chains.

- ***State Channels*:** Bitcoin uses payment channels, which enable exchange of Bitcoin transactions between two parties outside of the blockchain. Its Lightning Network technology implements Hashed Timelock Contracts (HTLCs), which are multi-party smart contracts,

---

[99] *"What is Sharding? Guide to this Ethereum Scaling Concept Explained"*, Blockonomi, July 2018.
[100] *"Ethereum Sharding Slated for 2020: ETH Foundation Researcher Justin Drake"*, CCN, July 2018.
[101] *"Zilliqa Mainnet: The Launch and Beyond"*, Zilliqa, January 2019.

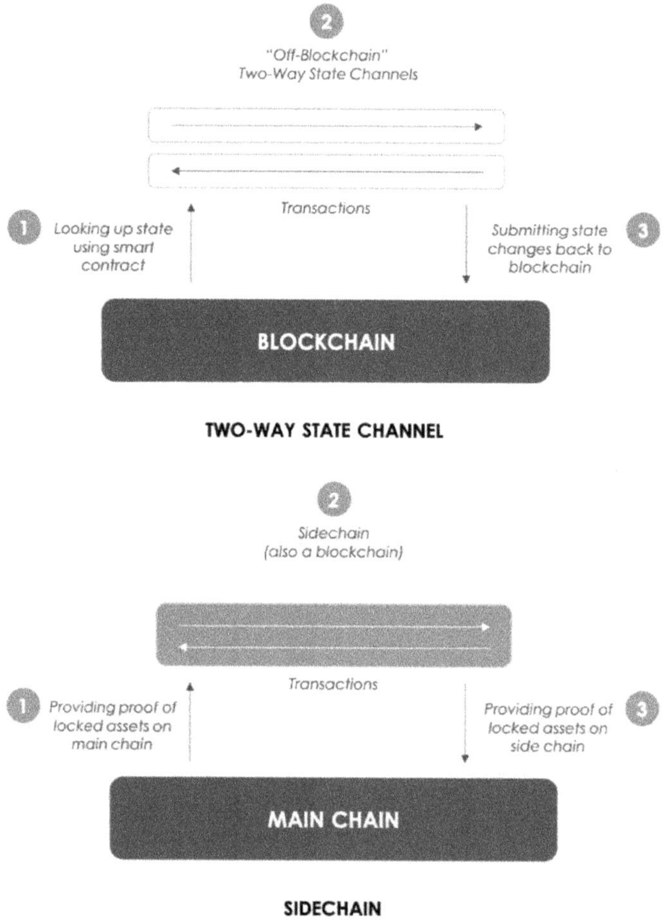

Figure 2.31. State Channels and Sidechain.

Source: *"Difference between Sidechains and State Channels"*, Vaibhav Saini, June 2018.

for scalability. A beta release of the Lightning Network was released in March 2018[102] and a year on, the Lightning Network has seen strong growth.[103] State channels are a more generic version of

[102] *"Bitcoin's Highly Anticipated Lightning Network Goes Live as Startup Raises $2.5M"*, Forbes, March 2018.

[103] *"Some Reflections on the One Year Anniversary of Bitcoin's Lightning Network"*, CryptoGlobe, March 2019.

payment channels used in Bitcoin. The Raiden Network is a Lightning-style network implementation in Ethereum, and went live on Ethereum in December 2018.[104] Beyond Lightning Network and Raiden Network, other examples of state channels include SpankChain, FunFair, Teechain, etc.[105]

- ***Side Chains***: Plasma is a technique used by Ethereum to achieve scalability, by the creation of "child" blockchains attached to the "main" Ethereum blockchain. Since the original conception in April 2017, there are evolutions to the Plasma concept, e.g. Plasma Cash[106] and other iterations.[107] However, development on Plasma has stalled, and zk-snarks is an emerging candidate for Ethereum scalability,[108] achieving 500 transactions per second in its testnet launch in January 2019.[109] Side chains are also one of the means to enable cross-chain interoperability, and this is discussed in Section 2.4.4.6 in "Blockchain Interoperability".

A combination of the above techniques is being developed and planned for Ethereum (see Table 2.6).

2.4.4.3.3 Alternative Distributed Ledgers

Directed Acyclic Graphs (DAGs) are emerging as potential solutions to overcome the scalability issues of "traditional" blockchains. At any point of time, a DAG can have an infinite number of tips (nodes at the very limit of the graph that are not yet referenced by other nodes), if we assume these nodes are transactions, it means an infinite number of transactions can be added to the graph at any point of time and can therefore be

---

[104] *"Red Eyes Mainnet Release Announcement"*, Raiden Network, December 2018.

[105] *"The State of State Channels: 2018 Edition"*, Dmitriy Berenzon, December 2018.

[106] *"Plasma Cash: New Scalability Solution for the Ethereum Network"*, Marco Cavicchioli, April 2018.

[107] *"Ethereum Transactions Fall Off the Cliff, Three Plasma Projects Close to Release Says Buterin"*, TrustNodes, July 2018.

[108] *"As Plasma Stalls, Snarks Becomes New Hope for Scaling Ethereum Now"*, CoinDesk, November 2018.

[109] *"ZCash Tech Fires Ethereum Towards True Scalability"*, CryptoBriefing, January 2019.

Table 2.6. Ethereum Roadmap.

Upgrade	Date	Details
Raiden Red Eyes	December 2018	Off-chain solution for faster and cheaper transactions.
Constantinople hard fork	January 2019	Lays the technical groundwork for significant scaling projects in the future.
Plasma	TBD	The introduction of "child" chains off the main Ethereum blockchain for faster and cheaper transactions. Similar to how the Lightning Network works on Bitcoin.
Casper	Mid 2019	Ethereum's main scaling goal. Casper is the shift from Proof-of-Work to the more efficient Proof-of-Stake.
Sharding	2020–2021	Partition the existing blockchain into smaller pieces known as shards.
Serenity (aka Ethereum 2.0)	2019–2021	The culmination of Casper and Sharding will create "Ethereum 2.0".
Ethereum 3.0	2022–2025	Implementation of a "super quadratic sharding" solution which could facilitate one billion transactions per day.

Source: *"The Future of Ethereum: A Scaling Roadmap to Casper, Plasma and Sharding"*, BlockExplorer, January 2019.

validated simultaneously if the network is large enough. In comparison, blockchain scalability is tied to the number of blocks that can be added per second and the number of transactions a given block can contain. A comparison of blockchain and DAG is shown in Table 2.7.

Key DAGs that are emerging include IOTA, Nano, ByteBall, TravelFlex, and IoT Chain.[110]

2.4.4.3.4 Customised Hardware

Another emerging development is the emergence of Application-Specific Integrated Circuit (ASIC)-based hardware for mining. Historically, users

[110] *"Top 5 Blockless Blockchain Projects Leveraging on DAG Technology"*, CryptoVerze, February 2019.

Table 2.7. Comparison of Blockchain and DAG.

Topic	Blockchain	DAG
Transaction validation	Each block references the previous one and blocks need to be added sequentially	• Each transaction verifies x previous transactions at the "tip" of the graph
Security	51% attack	• 33% attack • Additional weaknesses for non-regular hash function (IOTA)
Transaction/s	Hardcoded most of the time	• Virtually unlimited as the number of validating nodes grow
Scalability	Limited by the speed of the network to broadcast the full blockchain to all nodes	• Limited by the speed of the network to broadcast the full graph to the nodes • Limited by the size of the graph for IoT nodes with lower capacity

Source: *"Blockchain-less Technologies: Too Good to be True?"* Yacine Achiakh, July 2018.

mined Ethereum using GPUs; however, the emergence of ASICs for mining specific cryptocurrencies have resulted in a certain amount of centralisation as big players such as BitMain create higher barriers to entry for casual miners.[111]

To mitigate against the threat of centralised control over the cryptocurrency as a result of ASIC mining, some blockchains, such as the privacy-centric Monero, have been forking to gain ASIC resistance though a February 2019 report indicated 85% of the Monero network was dominated by ASIC miners.[112] Monero made subsequent protocol upgrades to enhance its PoW algorithm for improved ASIC resistance.[113] The Ethereum community also approved the implementation of the ASIC-resistant algorithm ProgPoW.[114]

---

[111] *"Ethereum Falls After Rumours of a Powerful Mining Chip Surface"*, TechCrunch, March 2018.

[112] *"Report Claims 85% of the Monero Network Dominated by ASIC Miners"*, Bitcoin.com, February 2019.

[113] *"Monero Upgrade Successful: Improved ASIC Resistance, Security, and Privacy"*, CryptoSlate, March 2019.

[114] *"Ethereum to Integrate ASIC-Resistant Algorithm ProgPow"*, FinanceMagnates, March 2019.

2.4.4.3.5 Enhancements on Consensus Algorithms

Researchers are also looking into enhancements of consensus algorithms, including AI-based consensus mechanisms. Proof of AI,[115] for example, uses a particular convolutional neural network and a dynamic threshold to arrive at consensus, and seeks to achieve similar performance results whilst mitigating the drawbacks of existing consensus algorithms (e.g. intensive network-wide computation, resulting in low throughput and high electrical consumption).

2.4.4.4 *Security and Privacy*[116]

2.4.4.4.1 Attacks on Blockchain Systems

51% attacks on blockchains are becoming a more regular occurrence, and Ethereum Classic, a top 20 crypto asset, was the target of such an attack in January 2019.[117] Smaller coins are more prone to such attacks as they attract fewer miners, so the cost to buy or rent the computing power necessary to build up a majority share of the network is lower. Mining marketplaces are also on the rise, lowering the barriers for attackers to gain access to mining hardware with lower hardware setup and investment cost.[118]

A research study suggests any blockchain with reasonably low transaction fees is vulnerable to 51% attacks.[119] Another industry article suggests that all the cryptocurrencies that use Proof-of-Work (PoW) are vulnerable to 51% attacks. These attacks are a serious risk to smaller

---

[115] *"An AI-Based Super Nodes Selection Algorithm in BlockChain Networks"*, Chen et al., August 2018.

[116] Note — Smart contract security issues will be covered in Section 2.4.4.5, under "Smart Contracts".

[117] *"ETC 51% Attack — What Happened and How It Was Stopped"*, BraveNewCoin, January 2019.

[118] *"Blockchain's Once-Feared 51% Attack is Now Becoming Regular"*, CoinDesk.com, June 2018.

[119] *"Rental Attacks Mean That Blockchains Must Evolve or Die"*, TechCrunch, July 2018.

cryptocurrencies, as it is economically feasible for attackers to rent sufficient mining power to launch such attacks.[120]

Besides 51% attacks, blockchains are also vulnerable to other attacks, including[121]:

- **Routing attack:** Made possible with the direct infiltration or cooperation of a key service provider operating within the blockchain ecosystem;
- **Sybil attack:** These attacks happen when a large number of nodes in a single network are owned by the same party; and
- **Direct denial of service:** These attacks are epitomised by flooding a system with high volume of requests and traffic to the server.

A research study examined and developed a taxonomy of blockchains' risks (see Table 2.8).

Table 2.8. Taxonomy of Blockchain's Risks.

Risk	**Cause**
51% vulnerability	Consensus mechanism
Private key security	Public-key encryption scheme
Criminal activity	Cryptocurrency application
Double spending	Transaction verification mechanism
Transaction privacy leakage	Transaction design flaw
Criminal smart contracts	Smart contract application
Vulnerabilities in smart contract	Program design flaw
Under-optimised smart contract	Program writing flaw
Under-priced operations	EVM design flaw

Source: *"A Survey on the Security of Blockchain Systems"*, Li et al., February 2018.

[120] *"Cryptocurrencies and the Critical Vulnerability of a 51% Attack"*, FinTech Futures, October 2019.

[121] *"Hacking Blockchains: Major Cybersecurity Attack Vulnerabilities to be Mindful For"*, BitCoinExchangeGuide.com, June 2018.

2.4.4.4.2 Mitigating Against Security Attacks

End Point/Wallet Security

This typically refers to the devices that individuals and businesses use to access blockchain-based services. Access to a blockchain requires both a public and private key, and one of the ways to obtain the private key is to attack the endpoint, or digital wallet, which is typically one of the weakest points in the entire system.

Digital wallets can either be (i) software wallets that are installed on the users' computers or mobile devices to store the user's public and private keys and to interface with the blockchain, or (ii) hardware wallets that store the user's private key offline on a hardware device, protected by a secure chip (or equivalent).

For enhanced security, there are cold wallets; these are completely offline wallets used for cold storage of cryptocurrencies and other digital assets on the blockchain, and only connect to the Internet to send and receive such digital assets. Another variant is paper wallets, which are just pieces of paper with a private key written on them.

Table 2.9 is a comparison of various Bitcoin wallets.

Trusted Execution Environment (TEE)

TEEs are isolated, secure processing environments to achieve secure remote computation. Intel Software Guard Extension (SGX), for example, is an architecture extension designed for application developers who are seeking to protect select code and data from disclosure or modification. The application code is placed into an enclave by special instructions and software made available to developers via the Intel SGX SDK. Several blockchain projects, including Microsoft CoCo Framework,[122] Enigma,[123] and Anquan,[124] have announced collaborations and partnerships with Intel. Apart from commercial solutions, open source projects for building TEE, such as Keystone,[125] also exist.

---

[122] *"Collaborating with Microsoft to Strengthen Enterprise Blockchains"*, Intel, August 2017.

[123] *"Enigma/Intel — For Immediate Release"*, Enigma, June 2018.

[124] *"The Business of Building a Better Blockchain"*, Asian Scientist, November 2018.

[125] https://keystone-enclave.org.

Table 2.9. Comparison of Bitcoin Wallets.

	Cold storage				**Hot wallets**						
	Hardware wallet			**Paper wallet**	**Mobile wallets**			**Desktop wallets**			**Web wallets**
Wallet	Ledger Nano S	Trezor	Keep key		Copay	Blockchain	Mycelium	Copay	Exodus	Jaxx	
Supported coins	Multiple	Multiple	Multiple		BTC, BCH	BTC, BCH, ETH	BTC	BTC, BCH	Multiple	Multiple	
Supported platforms					Desktop Android iOS	Web iOS Android	iOS Android	Desktop Android iOS	Desktop	Desktop Android iOS Web	
Multisig					Yes	No	No	Yes	No	No	

Source: *"Bitcoin Wallet Reviews and Comparison"*, 99Bitcoins, January 2019.

2.4.4.4.3 Smart Contract Security

Smart contract security is to be covered in Section 2.4.4.5.

2.4.4.4.4 Side Chain Security

Paragraph in Section 2.4.4.3.2 discusses side chains as a means of scaling blockchains through the creation of a separate blockchain that is attached to its parent blockchain. Pegged side chains are used to transfer assets between multiple blockchains. Side chains are responsible for their own security, and if there is insufficient mining power to secure a side chain, it could be compromised.[126] Research such as "Non-Interactive Proofs of Proofs of Work" (NiPoPoW) has been described as a big step forward in making side chains more secure, a roadblock that has stalled side chain technology.[127]

2.4.4.4.5 Security Frameworks

As blockchains start going into deployment, there is a need to develop the blockchain-equivalent of IT security frameworks and standards. One such example is the PwC China Digital Asset Wallet Security Rating System, which is a rating system used for the security assessment of digital wallets.[128]

Beyond security frameworks, Blockchain implementation security hardening guides[129] are starting to emerge, as are blockchain security audit and penetration testing services.[130]

---

[126] *"What are Sidechains?"* HackerNoon, January 2018.

[127] *"The Sidechains Breakthrough Almost Everyone in Bitcoin Missed"*, CoinDesk, January 2017.

[128] *"PwC China Digital Asset Wallet Security Framework"*, PwC, December 2018.

[129] *"Blockchain Implementation Security: A Hardening How-To"*, Pen Test Partners, August 2017.

[130] Examples: CertiK, ChainSecurity, Hosho.io.

2.4.4.4.6 Privacy

Public blockchains are open to anyone to join and participate in the network, and expose their records of transactions to the nodes in the network. This implies little to no privacy for transactions, which may not be desirable for many enterprise applications or sectors where privacy is a regulatory and legal imperative.

Research is ongoing to develop privacy on blockchains, and the key projects seen as forerunners in this area are Zcash and Monero.

Zcash uses the concept of zero-knowledge proof (ZKP) and applies them in the context of blockchains. The technology, zk-SNARKS, is a variation of the zero-knowledge technique[131] and it encrypts all transactional data that are stored on the network. This method verifies that the data being exchanged are accurate, but it does so without revealing all of the transaction details. zk-SNARKS was incorporated into Ethereum in September 2017 as part of its Byzantium upgrade[132] and is also seen as an emerging candidate for Ethereum scalability.[133]

Monero was launched in 2014 and was the product of a Bitcoin fork, but created with several anonymity features. Monero allows its users to have control over the privacy of their data by keeping transaction information completely anonymous within the blockchain through the use of ring signatures, ring confidential transactions, and a network of stealth addresses.

2.4.4.4.7 Privacy-Preserving Smart Contracts

Privacy-preserving smart contracts are to be covered in subsequent section "Smart Contracts".

---

[131] "*On Zero-Knowledge Proofs in Blockchains*", Argon Group, March 2018.

[132] "*Ethereum Upgrade Byzantium is Live, Verifies First ZK-Snark Proof*", CoinTelegraph, September 2017.

[133] "*As Plasma Stalls, Snarks Becomes New Hope for Scaling Ethereum Now*", CoinDesk, November 2018.

2.4.4.5 *Smart Contracts*

A smart contract is a collection of code and data (sometimes referred to as functions and state) that is deployed using cryptographically signed transactions on the blockchain network.[134] Some have described smart contracts as one of the most appealing features of blockchains that would enable more widespread blockchain adoption.[135] However, smart contracts are still relatively nascent and there are still many limitations, e.g. lack of development expertise, code flaws, security.[136]

The key areas of research in smart contracts are classified by a research study[137] into four categories:

- **Codifying issues:** These refer to challenges that are related to the development of smart contracts, e.g. difficulty of writing correct smart contracts, inability to modify or terminate smart contracts, lack of support to identify under-optimised smart contracts and complexity of programming languages.
- **Security:** These refer to bugs or vulnerabilities that an adversary might utilise to launch an attack, e.g. transaction-ordering vulnerability, timestamp dependency vulnerability, mishandled exception vulnerability, re-entrancy vulnerability, criminal smart contract activities, lack of trustworthy data feeds "oracles".
- **Privacy:** These refer to issues related to disclosing contracts information to the public, e.g. lack of transactional privacy, lack of data feeds privacy.
- **Performance:** These refer to issues that affect the ability of the blockchain systems to scale, e.g. sequential execution of smart contracts, dead code, gas-costly patterns.

---

[134] *"NISTIR 8202 Blockchain Technology Overview — Section 6 Smart Contracts"*, NIST, October 2018.

[135] *"Why Smart Contracts Will Bring Blockchain to the Masses"*, Dataconomy, November 2017.

[136] *"Ethereum's Smart Contracts are Full of Holes"*, MIT Technology Review, March 2018.

[137] *"Blockchain-Based Smart Contracts: A Systematic Mapping Study"*, Alharby. M. and van Moorsel. A., October 2017.

2.4.4.5.1 Facilitating Smart Contracts Creation

- ***Smart Contracts Templates*:** Some research efforts examine the design landscape of potential formats for storage and transmission of smart legal agreements, which could pave the way for standardised formats for defining and manipulating smart legal agreements.[138]
- ***Automated Generation of Smart Contracts*:** Others look into modeling approaches to automate the generation of smart contracts.[139]
- ***Smart Contract Tools and Marketplaces*:** Tools such as graphical smart contract editors are also emerging to make smart contracts easier to create. One such example is QuillPlay,[140] a smart contracts platform which would offer a drag-and-drop interface for smart contracts when launched. Vyper is another example — beta launched in June 2018, it is a Python-based language aimed at simplifying smart contract development with the objective of also targeting non-programmers.[141] As demand for smart contracts grow, this is paving the way for smart contract marketplaces, e.g. Modex, Dino, ContractVault.

2.4.4.5.2 Smart Contract Security

By simplifying the process of developing smart contracts and the creation of human-readable code, tools such as Vyper, mentioned above, also help to improve security in smart contracts and enable smart contract code auditability.

Vulnerabilities in Smart Contracts

Research has also been conducted on vulnerabilities in smart contracts (see Table 2.10).

---

[138] *"Smart Contract Templates: Essential Requirements and Design Options"*, Clack et al., December 2016.

[139] *"From Institutions to Code: Towards Automated Smart Contracts"*, Frantz, C., K. and Nowostawski, M., September 2016.

[140] https://www.quillhash.com/QuillPlay.

[141] *"Smart Contracts of the Future? Vyper and Plutus"*, BlockGeeks, July 2018.

Table 2.10. Vulnerabilities in Smart Contracts.

Number	Vulnerability	Cause	Level
1	Call to the unknown	The called function does not exist	Contract source code
2	Out-of-gas send	Fallback of the callee is executed	
3	Exception disorder	Irregularity in exception handling	
4	Type casts	Type-check error in contract execution	
5	Re-entrancy vulnerability	Function is re-entered before termination	
6	Field disclosure	Private value is published by the miner	
7	Immutable bug	Alter a contract after deployment	EVM bytecode
8	Ether lost	Send ether to an orphan address	
9	Stack overflow	The number of values in stack exceeds 2014	
10	Unpredictable state	State of the contract is changed before invoking	Blockchain mechanism
11	Randomness bug	Seed is biased by malicious miner	
12	Timestamp dependence	Timestamp of block is changed by malicious miner	

Source: "A Survey on the Security of Blockchain Systems", Li et al., February 2018.

Mitigating Against Smart Contracts Vulnerabilities

- ***Decentralised Application Security Project (DASP)*:** Projects such as the DASP have emerged to discover smart contract vulnerabilities.[142] It bears similarities to the Open Web Application Security Project (OWASP), and is an open and collaborative effort leveraging upon the community to list the top 10 vulnerabilities.
- ***Security Analysis, Audit and Optimisation Tools for Smart Contracts*:** Security analysis tools have also been developed to identify smart contracts with security issues. Research projects on smart contracts

[142] *"DASP Top 10 of 2018"*, DASP, 2018.

and security have yielded tools such as Oyente,[143] Maian[144] and Zeus.[145] The findings from these studies are summarised in Figure 2.32.

Open source projects, such as MythX,[146] have also emerged. MythX is a security analysis API for Ethereum smart contracts, and can be used by developers to build purpose-built Ethereum security tools.

Apart from open source projects, there are also startups emerging in smart contract security analysis and audit. Certik[147] offers a formal verification platform for smart contracts and blockchain ecosystems, Quantstamp is developing a new protocol for smart contract verification,[148] and Solidified[149] is offering a full-audit service for smart contracts through a platform for crowd-sourced review of smart contracts.

Organisations Promoting Smart Contract Security

Arising from the healthy growth and adoption of blockchain and smart contracts, industry alliances such as the Smart Contract Security Alliance[150] have also been formed to create and evaluate the security of smart contracts. The Chamber of Digital Commerce also formed the Smart Contracts Alliance[151] to help shape adoption, technology standards, and policy around smart contracts.

2.4.4.5.3 Privacy-Preserving Smart Contracts

As mentioned in Section 2.4.4.4 on "Security and Privacy", public blockchains are open to anyone to join and participate in the network, and expose their records of transactions to the nodes in the network. This

---

[143] *"Making Smart Contracts Smarter"*, Luu et al., October 2016.

[144] *"Finding the Greedy, Prodigal, and Suicidal Contracts at Scale"*, Nikolic et al., February 2018.

[145] *"Zeus: Analysing Safety of Smart Contract"*, Kalra et al., February 2018.

[146] https://mythx.io.

[147] https://certik.org.

[148] https://quantstamp.com.

[149] https://solidified.io.

[150] https://www.smartcontractsecurityalliance.com.

[151] https://digitalchamber.org/initiatives/smart-contracts-alliance/.

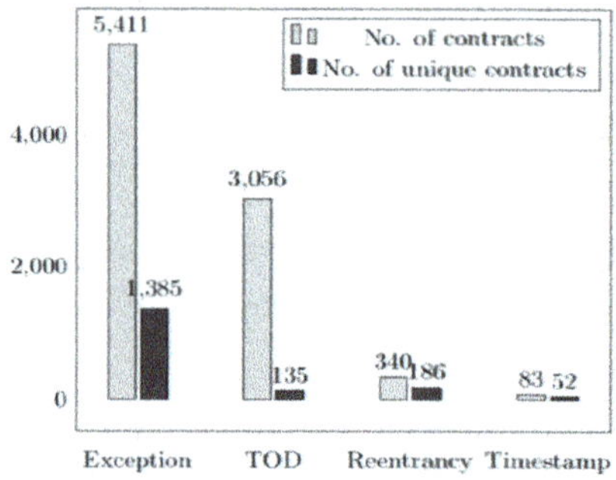

No of Buggy Contracts per Security Problem

- Run on all contracts in the first 1,459,999 blocks of Ethereum
- Of 19,366 smart contracts analysed (3,068,654 Ether), 8,833 smart contracts with at least 1 security issue flagged out

Maian

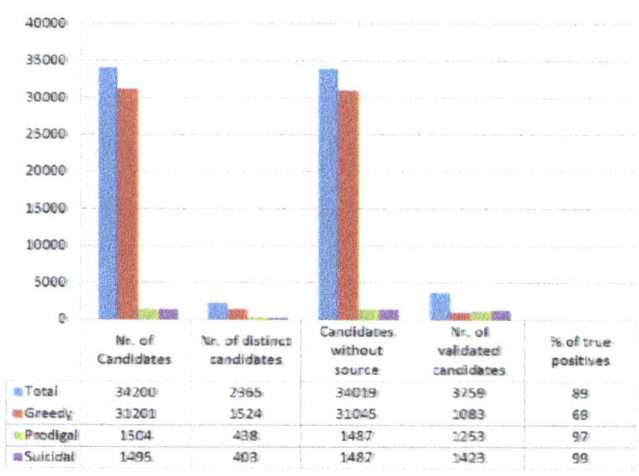

Results of Maian's Analysis of ~1M Smart Contracts

- Analysed 970,898 contracts
- 34,200 (2,365 distinct) contracts flagged

Zeus

Bug	ZEUS					
	Safe	Unsafe	No Result	Timeout	False +ve	False -ve
Reentrancy	1438	54	7	25	0	0
Unchkd. send	1191	324	5	4	3	0
Failed send	1068	447	3	6	0	0
Int. overflow	378	1095	18	33	40	0
Tx. State Dep.	1513	8	0	3	0	0
Blk. State Dep.	1266	250	3	5	0	0
Tx. Order Dep.	894	607	13	10	16	0

Zeus' Evaluation of Smart Contracts Vulnerabilities

- 21,281 out of 22,493 (or 94.6%) contracts containing more than $0.5 billion worth of Ether are vulnerable to one or more bugs

Figure 2.32. Findings from Security Analysis of Smart Contracts.

Source: *"Summary of Maian and its Million Contract Search for Vulnerabilities"*, Daniel Weiss, March 2018.

implies little to no privacy for transactions, which may not be desirable for many enterprise applications or sectors where privacy is a regulatory and legal imperative. Just as there is research ongoing to develop privacy on blockchains, there is also research looking into privacy-preserving smart contracts with the ability to hide inputs from everyone, except the person supplying it, perform some computation without revealing any state, and returning outputs based on the smart contract's specifications.

The approaches being explored include the following[152]:

- **Trusted Execution Environment (TEE):** This has been covered in Section 2.4.4.4 on "Security and Privacy";
- **Secure Multi-Party Computation (sMPC):** This cryptographic technique splits data into multiple pieces in a very specific way, and has individuals performing arithmetic operations on those pieces without revealing anything about the original data; and
- **Zero-Knowledge Proof (ZKP):** This has been covered in Section 2.4.4.4 on "Security and Privacy".

Examples of projects in the area of privacy-preserving smart contracts include Hawk,[153] Enigma[154] (their testnet was released in July 2018[155]), and Ekiden.[156]

2.4.4.5.4 AI-Powered Smart Contracts

While AI is currently not widely adopted for smart contracts, AI could potentially be applied to smart contracts in several ways, for example, evolving from rule-based systems such as expert systems designed to make decisions based on rules and input, to more adaptive systems, such as neural networks, knowledge graphs, and logic. AI and NLP could also

---

[152] *"Introduction to Privacy-Preserving Smart Contracts"*, Julian Koh, August 2018.

[153] *"Hawk: The Blockchain Model of Cryptography and Privacy-Preserving Smart Contracts"*, Kosba et al., May 2016.

[154] *"Defining Secret Contracts"*, Enigma, April 2018.

[155] *"The Code is Here — Announcing Enigma Testnet 1.0 Release"*, Enigma, July 2018.

[156] *"Ekiden: A Platform for Confidentiality-Preserving, Trustworthy, and Performant Smart Contract Execution"*, Cheng et al., July 2018.

be used with smart contracts in at least two aspects: to negotiate and agree to terms on behalf of people, and/or to generate the smart contracts. These contracts may be programmed to negotiate terms for price and quality of certain goods using well-known AI game playing algorithms. Parameters can be established for certain gap filler terms such as ranges of price and range of quality that can be adjusted dynamically, and fixed inputs by users for the type of goods.[157]

Early projects include Matrix, which incorporates blockchain and AI, e.g. natural language smart contracts[158] and Cortex, a decentralised AI platform that supports AI smart contracts and AI execution.[159]

2.4.4.6 *Blockchain Interoperability*

The current blockchain landscape is diverse, with many emerging players seeking to provide their respective unique public and private services. *Forbes* describes the verticalisation trend for blockchains for specific data and information recording uses, and suggests the need for a greater degree of connectivity between different blockchains.[160] The European Union Blockchain Observatory and Forum published a report[161] in March 2019, articulating how it sees blockchain evolving towards a global "backbone" of decentralised chains. The report suggests there are limitations of a multiverse of independent blockchains that cannot interoperate, and calls for blockchain interoperability standards.

The topics of blockchain interoperability can take on multiple dimensions, including:

- Interoperability between the blockchain and legacy systems;
- Interoperability between blockchain platforms; and
- Interoperability between two smart contracts within a single ledger.

---

[157] *"How AI will make Smart Contract "Smart""*, TechUK, April 2018.

[158] *"Matrix AI: New Chapter on Smart Contract with AI — Season 3"*, Hendrick J, September 2018.

[159] *"AI Smart Contracts — The Past, Present, and Future"*, Oscar W, November 2018.

[160] *"Blockchains are Verticalising, So We Need Interoperability"*, Forbes, February 2018.

[161] *"Scalability, Interoperability and Sustainability of Blockchains"*, EU Blockchain Observatory and Forum, March 2019.

Within the blockchain community, there is significant focus on interoperability between blockchain platforms (i.e. the second point), with several key methods for achieving interoperability, as well as emerging projects. The rest of this section in the publication will focus on interoperability between blockchain platforms.

2.4.4.6.1 Interoperability Technologies

The key blockchain interoperability technologies are classified by a research study[162] into four categories as follows:

- **Notary schemes:** In this mode, a trusted individual or group is used to declare to a blockchain that something has happened on another blockchain, or to make sure that the claim is correct. Interledger is an example of a project using a notary scheme[163];
- **Side chains/relays:** A side chain protocol is an agreement between two blockchains to achieve two-way peg, such that digital assets can be transferred between the main chain and the side chain.[164] Cosmos and PolkaDot are examples of projects using relay chain technologies[165];
- **Hash locking:** Hash locking is a trigger that sets interoperation between different blockchains, usually a hash of the random number to be discussed. The concept originated from Bitcoin's Lightning Network and uses Revocable Sequence Maturity Contract (RSMC) and Hash Time Locked Contract (HTLC) technologies. Its application scenario is more limited, in that it can achieve exchange of cross-chain assets, but not the transfer of cross-chain assets nor cross-chain contracts; and

[162] *"Research on Cross-Chain Technology Based on Sidechain and Hash-Lockin"*, Deng et al., June 2018.
[163] *"InterValue's Cross-Chain Technology and Multi-Chain Integration will Realise Value Interconnection"*, Intervalue, June 2018.
[164] Side chains are also discussed in Section 2.4.4.3 on "Network", in the context of network scalability.
[165] *"InterValue's Cross-Chain Technology and Multi-Chain Integration Will Realise Value Interconnection"*, Intervalue, June 2018.

- **Distributed private key control:** This uses a distributed private key generation and control technology to generate a locked account of the original chain and then maps the corresponding assets to its own blockchain.

Table 2.11 provides a comparison of some key cross-chain technologies described above.

Table 2.11. Comparison of Key Cross-Chain Technologies.

Cross-chain technology	**Notary technology**	**Side chain/relay technology**	**Hash locking technology**
Interoperability	All	All *Requires relaying on all chains, otherwise only one-way support*	Only cross-dependence
Trust model	Most notaries are honest	Chain will not fail or be attacked by 51%	Chain will not fail or be attacked by 51%
Suitability for cross-chain exchange	Support	Support	Support
Suitability for cross-chain asset transfer	Support *Requires common long-term notary support*	Support	Do not support
Suitability for cross-chain prediction machine	Support	Support	Not directly supported
Suitability for cross-chain asset mortgage	Support *Requires common long-term notary support*	Support	Supported but with difficulty

Source: *"InterValue's Cross-Chain Technology and Multi-Chain Integration Will Realise Value Interconnection"*, Intervalue, June 2018.

2.4.4.6.2 Blockchain Interoperability Projects

There are many blockchain interoperability projects,[166] including Polkadot, Cosmos, ICON, Wanchain, Fusion, and Block Collider. A comparison of some of these projects are shown in Table 2.12.

Figure 2.33 presents these blockchain interoperability projects from the perspective of their scope and methods of interoperability.

2.4.4.6.3 Organisations Promoting Blockchain Interoperability

Some of these cross-chain projects have also come together to evolve blockchain technology and interoperability. For example, Aion, Wanchain, and ICON have come together to form the Blockchain Interoperability Alliance (BIA), with Wanchain taking an active interest in the Chinese market, ICON in the South Korean market, and AION in the North American market.[167]

2.4.4.7 *Post-Quantum Blockchain*

Quantum computers are powerful machines that take a new approach, built on the principles of quantum mechanics, to processing information.[168] Quantum computing technologies have been advancing very rapidly, and their strong processing capabilities pose a threat to the cryptographic technologies that underpin the security properties of blockchains.

A blockchain is secured by two major mechanisms: (i) encryption via asymmetric cryptography and (ii) hashing.

---

[166] *"The Race for Cross-Chain Communication: 11 Projects Working on Blockchain Interoperability"*, InvestInBlockchain, July 2018.
[167] *"Blockchain Interoperability Alliance (BIA) — Defining Blockchain 3.0"*, CryptoVest, February 2018.
[168] *"What is Quantum Computing"*, IBM, 2018.

Table 2.12. Interoperability Protocols — The Current Landscape.

Features	Block Collider	Polkadot	Cosmos	Ark	ICON	Wanchain	Aion	Cardano
Consensus Algorithm	PoD (Proof-of-Distance)	DPoS (Delegated Proof-of-Stake)	Tendermint BFT (Byzantine Fault Tolerance)	DPoS (Delegated Proof-of-Stake)	LFT (Loop Fault Tolerance)	PoS (Proof-of-Stake)	DPoS (Delegated Proof-of-Stake) & PoI (Proof-of-Intelligence)	Ouroboros PoS (Proof-of-Stake)
Interoperability Technology	Multichain Weaving	Relaychain and Parachains / Multichain of Parachains	Notary Scheme	Notary Scheme	Notary Scheme	Notary Scheme	Notary Scheme	Notary Scheme
Validators	Not required	Required	Required	Required	Required	Required	Required	Required
Number of Validators	None required	Number of validators undefined in whitepaper	100 Validators (Cosmos Hub). This number will increase at a rate of 13% for 10 years, and settle at 300 validators	51 Delegates	Number of validators undefined in whitepaper (No indicator yet that there is an upper limit)	Unbound	Number of validators undefined in whitepaper (No indicator yet that there is an upper limit)	Unbound

Interoperability Keyword	Collision (PoD) mined into one multi-chain	Parachains (Member chains) Bridgechains (For non-compatible chains)	Cosmos Hub and Zones (Member chains) Peg-zones (For non-compatible chains)	Smartbridge Encode Listener Nodes (Existing chains)	Icon Republic and Communities where nodes act as witnesses	Cross-chain Transaction Data Transmission Module where nodes act as witnesses	Connecting Networks and Bridges in the form of Side chains	Federated Bridges in the form of Side chains
Participating Chain Conditions	No conditions to join network	Member chains require compatibility Non-compatible chains can utilise Bridgechains	Member chains require compatibility Non-compatible chains can utilise Peg-Zones	Member chains require compatibility Non-compatible chains can utilise Encode Listener nodes	No conditions to join network	No conditions to join network	No conditions to join network	No conditions to join network
Value Transfer	Yes	Yes	Yes	Yes	Yes	Yes – Additionally designed for asset portability	Yes	Yes

(Continued)

Table 2.12. (*Continued*)

Access to Data — States of Member Chains	Full state of member chains as part of the protocol's data	Full state of member chains as part of the protocol's data (Not applicable to bridge chains)	Verifying the state based on verification by a validator	Verifying the state based on verification by a validator	Verifying the state based on verification by a validator	Verifying the state based on verification by a validator	Verifying the state based on verification by a validator	Verifying the state based on verification by a validator
Scalability for Member Chains	Does not provide scalability for member chains	Provides scalability solution for member chains Does not provide scalability for chains utilising Bridgechains	Provides scalability solution for member chains Does not provide scalability for chains utilising Peg-zones	Does not provide scalability for member chains	Does not provide scalability for member chains	Does not provide scalability for member chains	Does not provide scalability for member chains	Does not provide scalability for member chains

Shared Security for Member Chains	Does not provide shared security for member chains	Provides shared security solution for member chains Does not provide shared security for chains utilising Bridgechains	Provides shared security solution for member chains Does not provide shared security for chains utilising Peg-zones	Does not provide shared security for member chains	Does not provide shared security for member chains	Does not provide shared security for member chains	Does not provide shared security for member chains	Does not provide shared security for member chains

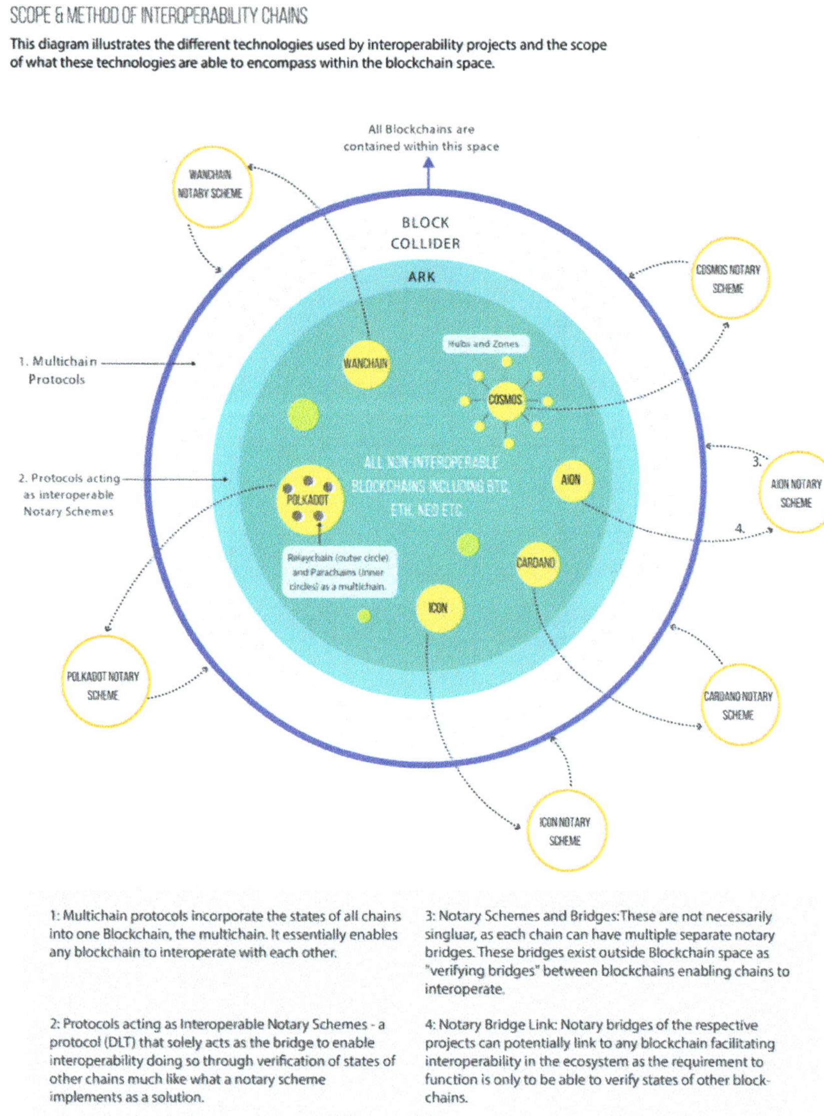

Figure 2.33. Scope and Method of Interoperability Chains.
Source: *"Interoperability Overview"*, Spec-Retionality.com, 2019.

2.4.4.7.1 Shor's Algorithm — Impact on Asymmetric Cryptography[169]

The public and private keys used to secure blockchain transactions are both very large numbers, hashed into a group of smaller numbers. Asymmetric cryptography algorithms depend on computers being unable to find the prime factors of these enormous numbers.

Shor's algorithm is a quantum algorithm optimised to solve for prime factors. Using the most common encryption standard, it takes a classical computer 2128, that is to say 340,282,366,920,938,463,463,374,607,431, 768,211,456 basic operations, to find the private key associated with a public key. On a quantum computer, it would take 1283 (i.e. only 2,097,152) basic operations to find the private key associated with a public key.

Elliptic curve digital signatures, which form the foundation of current blockchain security, are vulnerable to Shor's algorithm.[170]

2.4.4.7.2 Grover's Algorithm — Impact on Hashing[171]

Grover's algorithm is a quantum algorithm that allows a user to search through an unordered list for specific items. It requires 2256 (which is a 78-digit number) of basic operations with a classical computer to find the correct hash. For a quantum computer using Grover's Algorithm, it would only take 2128 (which is a 39-digit number, broken out above in the Shor's Algorithm section) of basic operations to solve for the correct hash.

Recognising that the quantum era is near, there is active research ongoing in the area of blockchains to ensure their security properties are not compromised, even in the quantum era.

---

[169] *"Quantum Threat to Blockchains: Shor's and Grover's Algorithms"*, Shaan Ray, July 2018.

[170] *"The Case for a Quantum Resistant Ledger"*, Jomari Peterson, April 2017.

[171] *"Quantum Threat to Blockchains: Shor's and Grover's Algorithms"*, Shaan Ray, July 2018.

2.4.4.7.3 Quantum-Proofing New Blockchains

Using Post-Quantum Cryptographic Schemes

Designing quantum-resistant blockchains from scratch would involve the application of post-quantum cryptographic schemes and quantum cryptography.

In 2016, the US National Institute for Standards and Technology (NIST) initiated a multi-year standardisation project to identify candidate quantum-resistant cryptosystems. It cites[172] estimates made by Dr Michele Mosca, University of Waterloo, that:

> "There is a 1 in 7 chance that some fundamental public-key crypto will be broken by quantum by 2026, and a 1 in 2 chance of the same by 2031."

NIST has shortlisted 26 potential algorithms that could potentially be quantum-resistant,[173] and draft NIST standards for quantum-resistant cryptographic algorithms are estimated to be ready in 2023–2025.[174]

The most cost-effective way of making the blockchain resistant against quantum attacks is to replace the currently deployed digital signature schemes, which are based on RSA or EC-DSA, with post-quantum ones. Examples of post-quantum schemes are lattice-based schemes (learning with errors, LWE), super singular isogenies schemes, multivariate-polynomial schemes, code-based schemes, or Merkle tree-based signatures.[175]

Blockchains Using Quantum Cryptography[176]

Quantum cryptographic tools may also be used to make blockchains more secure. Examples include:

---

[172] *"The Ship Has Sailed: The NIST Post-Quantum Cryptography Competition"*, NIST, December 2017.

[173] *"NIST Reveals 26 Algorithms Advancing to Post-Quantum Crypto "Semifinals""*, NIST, January 2019.

[174] *"Update on NIST Post-Quantum Cryptography Project"*, NIST.

[175] *"Quantum-Proofing the Blockchain"*, Gheorghiu et al., November 2017.

[176] *Ibid.*

- **Quantum Random Number Generators (QRNGs):** They avoid the cryptanalytic risks associated with pseudo-random number generators, and promise a more fundamental and more reliable source of randomness than conventional entropy-based random number generators;
- **Quantum Key Distribution (QKD) Systems:** This is a method for using an untrusted quantum channel to establish symmetric keys through an untrusted, but authenticated, communication channel. This is what is often achieved today using public key-based key agreement authenticated by public key signatures, and can be achieved in the future using post-quantum public key schemes; and
- Other quantum tools, e.g. quantum authentication, quantum money, quantum fingerprints.

Quantum-resistant blockchain projects have already been announced, e.g. Russian Quantum Centre in Moscow indicated they had developed the world's first quantum-proof blockchain,[177] Quantum Resistant Ledger by the QRL Foundation was launched in June 2018.[178] Ethereum is also said to achieve quantum resistance around 2022–2024.[179]

Quantum-Proofing Existing Blockchains

Replacement of Vulnerable Algorithms. Patching existing blockchains against quantum attacks may be significantly harder than designing quantum-safe blockchains from scratch. The first step is to replace the vulnerable cryptographic primitives with quantum-resistant ones. For example, in the Bitcoin network, there is a need to replace the digital signature scheme with a quantum-resistant scheme and use the latter to sign new transactions. This approach would provide security for future transactions.[180]

---

[177] *"Scientists Claim to have Invented the World's First Quantum-Proof Blockchain"*, ScienceAlert, May 2017.

[178] *"QRL Launches Quantum Resistant Blockchain"*, BlockchainNews, June 2018.

[179] *"Ethereum Core Researcher Targets Quantum Resistance Date, Dials in Timeframe for Upcoming 2.0 Launch"*, DailyHODL.com, April 2019.

[180] *"Quantum-Proofing the Blockchain"*, Gheorghiu et al., November 2017.

Specific to Bitcoin, there is also research to examine the risk of Bitcoin to attacks by quantum computers, with findings indicating that the Proof-of-Work used by Bitcoin is relatively resistant to substantial speedup by quantum computers in the next 10 years; however, the elliptic curve signature scheme used by Bitcoin is much more at risk and could be completely broken by a quantum computer as early as 2027. The same research study also reviewed available post-quantum signature schemes, suggesting candidates that would best meet the security and efficiency requirements of blockchain applications hash and lattice-based schemes (see Table 2.13).

Table 2.13. Comparison of Public Key and Signature Lengths of Post-Quantum Signature Schemes in kilobits (kb).

Type	Name	Security level (bits)	PK length (kb)	Sig. length (kb)	PK + Sig. lengths (kb)
I.1	GPV	100	300	240	540
I.2	LYU	100	65	103	168
I.3	BLISS	128	7	5	12
I.4	DILITHIUM	138	11.8	21.6	33.4
II.1	RAINBOW	160	305	0.244	305
III.1	LMS	128	0.448	20	20.5
III.2	XMSS	128	0.544	20	20.5
III.3	SPHINCS	128	8	328	336
III.4	NSW	128	0.256	36	36
IV.1	CFS	83	9216	0.1	9216
IV.2	QUARTZ	80	568	0.128	568

Note: The security level given is against classical attacks. Type I are lattice based, type II based on multivariate polynomials, type III hashing based, and type IV code based.

Source: *"Quantum Attacks on Bitcoin, and How to Protect Against Them"*, Aggarwal et al., October 2017.

Secure Transition Strategies. Research is also ongoing to examine secure transition strategies for existing blockchains, e.g. a commit-delay-reveal approach where a sufficiently long delay period of six months is proposed for consensus to be reached.[181]

2.4.4.8 *Standards Development*

RAND Europe was commissioned by the British Standards Institute (BSI) to examine the potential role of standards in supporting blockchain, and the key areas where standards could play a role in supporting blockchain, as well as the indicative time frame are shown in Figure 2.34.

2.4.5 *Technology Roadmap*

Table 2.14 reflects industry's view on the likely evolution and mainstream adoption of blockchain technology as of publication of the IMDA Services and Digital Economy (SDE) Technology Roadmap in November 2018.

[181] *"Committing to Quantum Resistance: A Slow Defence for Bitcoin Against a Fast Quantum Computing Attack"*, Stewart et al., 2018.

Summary box: Key points related to the prospective role of standards to support DLT/Blockchain

- Standards could play an important role in ensuring interoperability between multiple DLT/Blockchain implementations and, in doing so, could help reduce the risk of a fragmented ecosystem.
- Using standards to establish a stronger consensus on consistent terminology and vocabulary could improve understanding of the technology and help progress the market.
- Establishing standards to address the security and resilience of, and the privacy and data governance concerns related to DLT/Blockchain could help create trust in the technology.
- Standards could play a role in digital identity management and foster end-user trust in the technology.
- There are potential opportunities for standards to play a role in sectors where provenance tracking is important.
- It may be too early to think about standards related to the technical aspects of DLT/Blockchain.

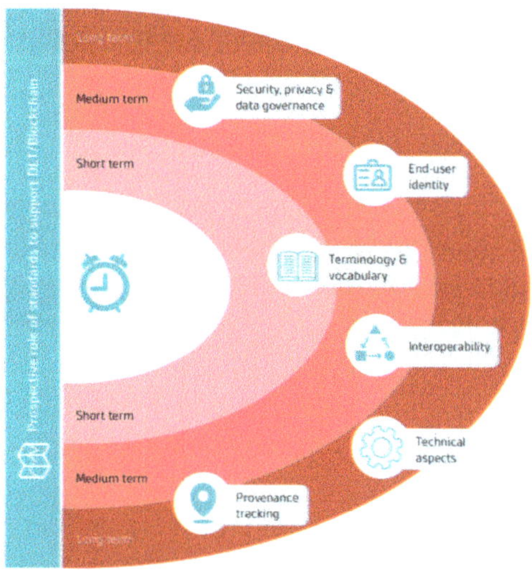

Source: RAND Europe

Figure 2.34. Role of Standards in Supporting Blockchain.

Source: *"Distributed Ledger Technologies/Blockchain: Challenges, Opportunities, and the Prospects for Standards"*, British Standards Institution (NSI) and RAND Europe, May 2017.

Table 2.14. Likely Evolution and Mainstream Adoption of Blockchain Technology.

	Now–2 Years	**3–5 Years**	**> 5 Years**
Governance			
Governance mechanisms & strategies		• Off-chain governance mechanisms	• On-chain governance • New governance strategies, e.g. futarchy, liquid democracy, quadrating voting
Emerging multi-disciplinary areas			
Multi-Disciplines		• Crypto-economics • "Lex cryptographia"	
Network — Improvement in scalability & throughput[a]			
Data structure	• Increase block size, e.g. Segwit – Segwit v1[b] – Segwit2x hard fork[c]	• New data structures, e.g. Directed Acyclic Graphs (DAGs), e.g. – Hashgraph – SPECTRE – IOTA – ByteBall	
Layer 1	<u>Consensus</u> • Proof-of-Work • Proof-of-Stake[d] <u>Sharding</u> Implementation of sharding in blockchains, e.g. Zilliqa (2018)	<u>Consensus</u> • Proof-of-Stake <u>Sharding</u> Implementation of sharding in key blockchains, e.g. Ethereum over two phases, in 2020 and 2021	<u>Consensus</u> Enhancements in consensus algorithms, e.g. AI-based consensus

(Continued)

Table 2.14. (*Continued*)

	Now–2 Years	**3–5 Years**	**> 5 Years**
Layer 2	State Channels Implementation of state channels in blockchains, e.g. • Bitcoin — Lightning Network beta[e] • Raiden Network launch[f] Side Chains Implementation of side chains, e.g. Plasma Cash initial release[g] E.g. Plasma Cash initial release (June 2018)	State Channels Bitcoin — Lightning Network Ethereum — Raiden Network Side Chains Plasma	
Hardware	GPU & ASIC hardware for mining	ASIC-resistant consensus, e.g. Monero	
Tokenisation			
Tokenisation	Feature Development In enterprise blockchains, e.g. UTXO[h] token for Fabric included in January 2018 Hyperledger Fabric paper	Feature Development In enterprise blockchains, e.g. UTXO token for Hyperledger Fabric Application Tokenisation of assets	
Security and privacy			
Network security		Network Security • Hardware trusted execution environment End-User Security • Software wallets • Hardware wallets	Network Security • Side chain security

Security frameworks/ guidelines	• Emergence of – Blockchain implementation hardening guides – Pen testing – Blockchain security framework, e.g. Digital Asset Wallet Security Framework	• Blockchain security frameworks and guides, e.g. hardening • Blockchain security analysis and testing tools, e.g. pen testing • Commercial blockchain security services, e.g. audit services	
Privacy	• zk-SNARKS implemented in Ethereum in September 2017 • Ring signature introduced as optional feature to Monero in January 2017, made mandatory in September 2017	• zk-SNARKS • Ring signature • Secret sharing, threshold secret sharing, secure multi-party computation (MPC)	• Side chain privacy
Smart contracts			
Codification	• Tools to simplify smart contract programming emerging, e.g. Vyper, EtherScripter	• Graphical smart contract editors	• Cognitive smart contracts
Security	• Smart contract security analysis research & tools, e.g. – Oyente (2016) – Maian (2018) – Mythril (2017) – Zeus (2018)	• Smart contract security analysis, e.g. – Frameworks and guidelines – Tools – Commercial services, e.g. audit	
Privacy	• Privacy-preserving smart contracts, e.g. – Hawk (2016) – Ekiden (2018) – Enigma secret contracts (1.0 in 2018, 2.0 in 2019)	• Privacy-preserving smart contract protocols & platforms	

(Continued)

Table 2.14. *(Continued)*

	Now–2 Years	**3–5 Years**	**> 5 Years**
Performance	• Smart contract optimisation review services — Built into some smart contract security audit services	• Smart contract optimisation – Tools – Commercial services	
Interoperability			
Notary schemes	E.g. Interledger protocol		• Interoperable blockchains • Transition – Frameworks and guidelines – Tools – Commercial services
Sidechains/relays	E.g. Cosmos, Polkadot, Block Collider		
Hash locking	Hashed Time Locked Contract		
Distributed parent key control	E.g. Wanchain, Fusion		
Post-quantum blockchain			
Quantum-resistant blockchains			• Post-quantum signature schemes • Blockchains using quantum cryptography, e.g. – Quantum Random Number Generators (RNGs) – Quantum Key Distribution (QKD) systems – Other quantum tools
Quantum-proofing existing blockchains			• Replacement of vulnerable algorithms • Secure transition strategies – Methodologies and guidelines – Tools – Commercial services

Standards development			
Standards	• Terminology and vocabulary	• Security, privacy and data governance • End-user identity • Interoperability	• Provenance tracking

Note: [a]Primarily applicable to public blockchains.

[b]Integrated into Bitcoin network late 2017.

[c]Subsequently called off.

[d]Transition for Ethereum expected in 2019.

[e]March 2018.

[f]Summer 2018.

[g]June 2018.

[h]Unspent Transaction Output.

Chapter 3

Convergence of AI, Data and Blockchain

3.1 Law of Accelerating Returns and Technological Convergence

Ray Kurzweil, a futurist, suggests that the rate of change in a wide variety of evolutionary systems (including but not limited to the growth of technologies) tends to increase exponentially.[1] One of the drivers for this lies in technological convergence, as technologies "stack up" over other technologies to augment one another. This is consistent with suggestions from other futurists, such as Geon Leonhard who suggests that the future is exponential and combinatorial.[2] Frank Diana suggests that disruptive power lies at the intersections[3] (see Figure 3.1).

Deloitte's report on exponential innovation also suggests that as boundaries blur and dissolve, exponential innovation cannot be fully described by examining any single technology or sector. Focusing on only one technology or sector can miss the broader impacts and opportunities driven by these converging technologies. It is from their interaction and often-unexpected configurations and reconfigurations that radically new innovations — and disruptions — are emerging.[4]

---

[1] *"Law of Accelerating Returns"*, Ray Kurzweil, March 2001.

[2] *"Futurist Keynote Speaker Gerd Leonhard LT15 Excerp"*, YouTube, 2015.

[3] *"Intersections Promise to Drive Multiple Paradigm Shifts"*, Frank Diana, February 2017.

[4] *"From Exponential Technologies to Exponential Innovation"*, Deloitte University Press, 2013.

Figure 3.1. Intersections Amplify Both Power and Impact.

Source: *"The Latest Exponential and Combinatorial Illustration of What the Future Will Bring"*, Gerd Leonhard, April 2016.

To this end, beyond examining individual technologies such as AI and blockchain, there is also a need to understand the areas of convergence and intersection across AI, data and blockchain.

3.2 Convergence of AI, IoT, and Blockchain

As shown in Figure 3.2, the convergence of blockchain, IoT, and AI can enable organisations to maximise the benefits of each of these technologies while minimising the risks and limitations associated with them. As IoT networks comprise a myriad of connected devices, there are numerous vulnerabilities in the network, leaving it prone to hacker attacks, fraud, and data theft. To prevent security issues, AI powered by machine learning can proactively defend against malware and hacker attacks. The security of the network and the data can be further enhanced by blockchain, which can limit illicit access and modification of the data on the network. AI can also enhance the functional capability of the IoT network by making it smarter and more autonomous.[5]

[5] *"What Happens when Blockchain, IoT, and AI Converge"*, Allerin, October 2018.

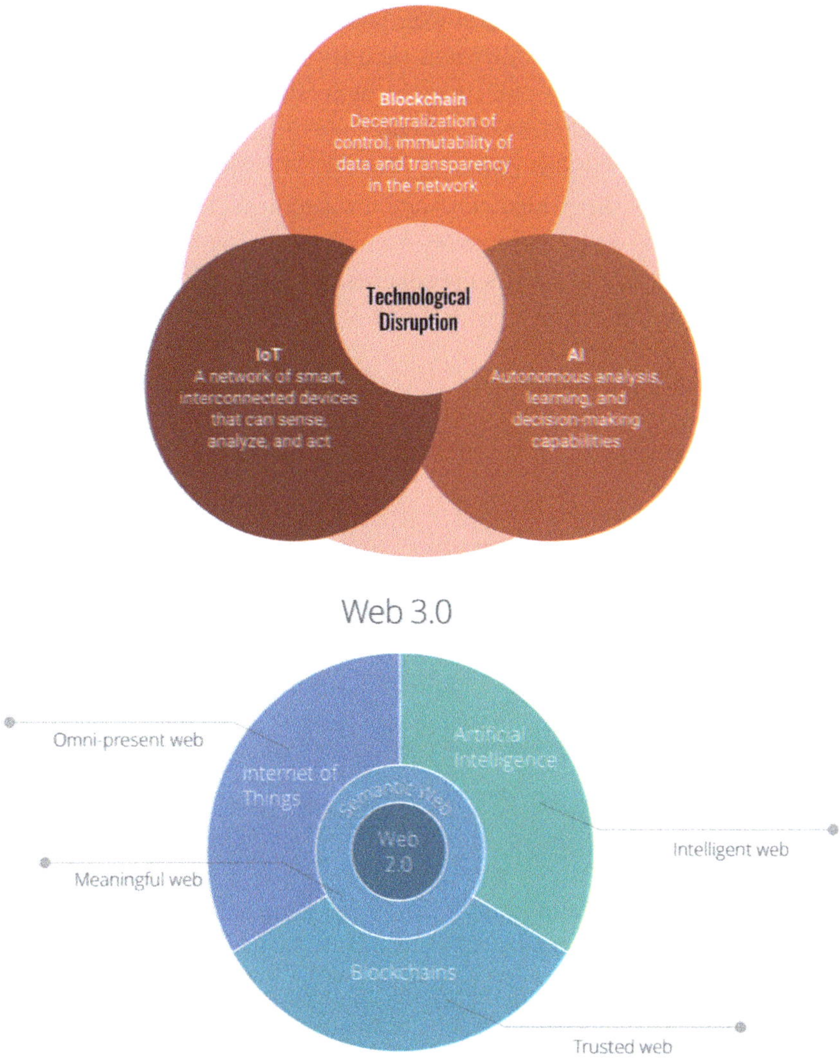

Figure 3.2. Convergence of AI, IoT and Blockchain.

Source: *"What Happens when Blockchain, IoT, and AI Converge"*, Allerin, October 2018.

3.2.1 *Blockchain and IoT*

IoT has the potential to connect billions of objects simultaneously, which has the impact of improving information-sharing needs that result in improving our life. Although there are many benefits to IoT, there are also deployment challenges in the real world due to its centralised server/client model. For instance, scalability and security issues that arise due to the excessive numbers of IoT objects in the network. The server/client model requires all devices to be connected and authenticated through the server, which creates a single point of failure. Blockchain enables the decentralisation of the computation and management processes which can solve many of IoT issues, especially security.

A research study examines the benefits of integrating blockchain with IoT.[6] It cites the following as benefits of blockchain with IoT:

- Decentralisation;
- Resiliency;
- Security;
- Speed;
- Cost saving;
- Immutability;
- Anonymity; and
- Publicity.

The study also acknowledges the challenges that still need to be addressed:

- Scalability;
- Storage;
- Processing power and time;
- Naming and discovery;
- Lack of skills; and
- Legal and compliance.

Forbes suggests that blockchain could be the way to save IoT,[7] whilst *ComputerWorld* suggests that IoT could be the killer app for blockchains.[8]

---

[6] *"Blockchain with Internet of Things: Benefits, Challenges, and Future Directions"*, Atlam et al., June 2018.

[7] *"Is Blockchain the Way to Save IoT?"* Forbes, July 2018.

[8] *"IoT Could Be the Killer App for Blockchain"*, ComputerWorld, June 2018.

Regardless, blockchain/IoT players have since emerged, leveraging the complementary nature of these two technology areas to develop products and solutions.[9] Examples of early players include Filament Networks,[10] which offers an end-to-end solution that enables self-forming wireless mesh networks over long-range radio, and IOTA,[11] a blockchain-based transactional settlement and data transfer layer for IoT. In Singapore, players such as VeChain[12] have also emerged, leveraging blockchain and IoT to target use cases in the supply chain.

3.2.2 *Blockchain and AI*

Forbes suggests that there are three major benefits of combining AI and blockchain[13]:

- AI and encryption work very well together;
- Blockchain can help us to track, understand, and explain decisions made by AI; and
- AI can manage blockchains more efficiently than humans.

A IEEE Computer Society article suggests that blockchain will bring trustlessness, privacy, and explainability to AI; in turn, AI can help build a machine learning system on blockchain for better security, scalability, and more effective personalisation and governance:

3.2.2.1 *Blockchain for AI*

Just as in the case of blockchain and IoT, players leveraging on the complementary characteristics of AI and Blockchain have already emerged. For example, early players leveraging blockchain to enable

---

[9] *"Blockchains and the IoT"*, Postscapes, August 2018.
[10] https://filament.com.
[11] https://www.iota.org.
[12] https://www.vechain.org.
[13] *"Artificial Intelligence and Blockchain: 3 Major Benefits of Combining These 2 Mega-Trends"*, Forbes, March 2018.

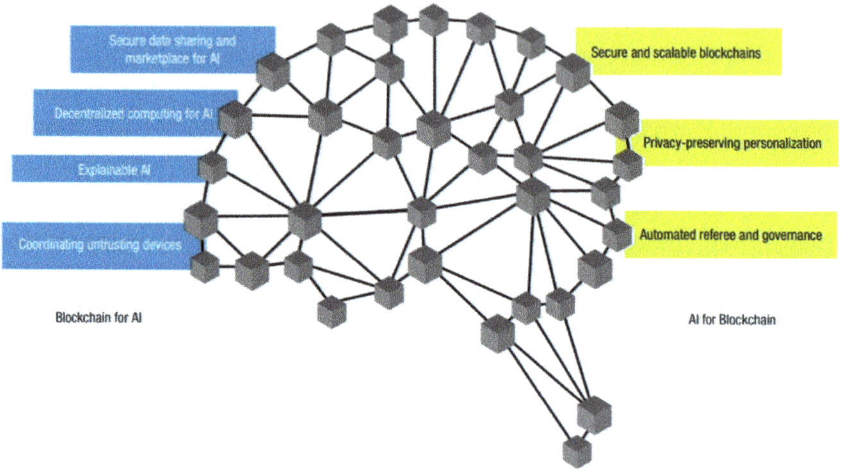

Figure 3.3. The Integration of Blockchain and AI.

Source: *"AI and Blockchain: A Disruptive Integration"*, Thang N. Dinh and My T. Thai, "Computer", IEEE Computer Society, September 2018.

secure data sharing and marketplaces for AI include Enigma[14] and SingularityNet.[15] This convergence has resulted in the use of the phrase "decentralised AI", and the emergence of industry bodies such as the Decentralised AI Alliance to foster the development of decentralised AI technologies (see Figure 3.3).

3.2.2.2 *AI for Blockchain*

As in Figure 3.4, AI can also enable blockchain technology and implementation. For example, the application of AI to enhance the consensus mechanism in blockchain was discussed in Section 3.4.3 and the application of AI in AI-powered smart contracts was discussed in Section 3.4.5. Another research looks into the application of AI in smart contract testing. The same research study suggests the application of the

---

[14] https://enigma.co.

[15] https://singularitynet.io.

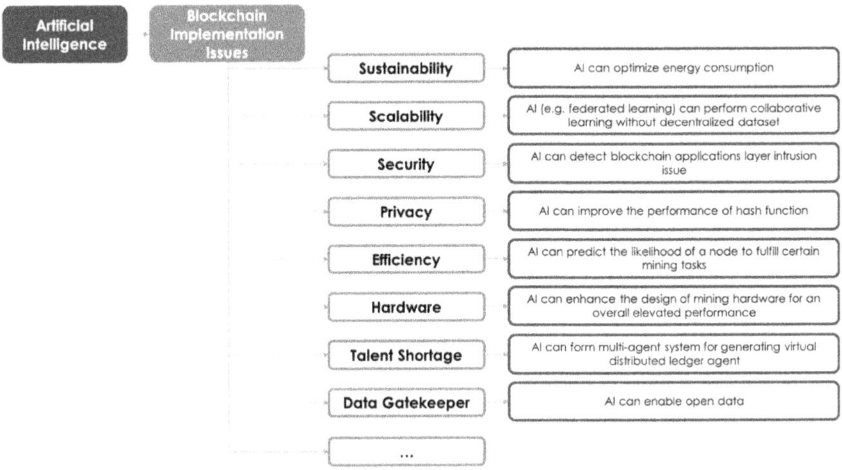

Figure 3.4. The Synergy of AI and Blockchain.

Source: *"Blockchain and Artificial Intelligence"*, Marwala, T. and Bo. X, February 2018.

following framework to examine the application of AI in blockchain implementation.

3.3 Convergence of AI, Blockchain, and Cybersecurity

As the sophistication of cyberattacks on enterprises, Governments, and individuals increase around the world, it is increasingly clear that organisations may not be able to solely rely on manpower and human interaction to ward of cyberattacks, and there is a need to explore new means to boost cyber defences. Convergence has been described as the future of cybersecurity, as AI, edge analytics, predictive and reactive analytics, machine learning algorithms, and wireless features like RFID create new opportunities for organisations to take on a unified approach to proactively address the cybersecurity threats.[16]

[16] *"The Future of Cybersecurity is Convergence"*, Brilliance Security Magazine, May 2018.

3.3.1 *AI and Cybersecurity*

Amongst the technologies listed, AI is increasingly being looked at in the context of cybersecurity, and is expected to underpin cybersecurity in the next few years.[17]

Forbes suggests the following AI applications for cybersecurity[18]:

- **Biometric logins:** AI systems can scan fingerprints, retina, and palm prints accurately for biometric logins;
- **Detecting threats and malicious activities:** Cybersecurity firms are training AI systems to detect malware and viruses with the help of several datasets that include algorithms and codes;
- **Learning with natural language processing:** AI-powered systems can automatically collect data by scanning articles, studies, and news about cyber threats and select useful information with natural language processing; and
- **Securing conditional access:** AI-powered systems can help create a dynamic, real-time, and global authentication framework that alters access privileges based on location or network.

Table 3.1 gives further examples of major categories of cybersecurity threats, and the application of AI to mitigate these threats.

However, a recent NIST study also showed that whilst there is potential to apply machine learning in cybersecurity, currently, there are still some limitations.[19] *MIT Technology Review* also suggests that whilst machine learning and AI can help guard against cyberattacks, hackers can also foil security algorithms by targeting the data they train on and the warning flags they look for. As such, it is critical for security companies, and their customers, to monitor and minimise the risks associated with algorithmic models.[20] In a similar vein, ZDNet suggests that given the

[17] *"How AI will Underpin Cyber Security in the Next Few Years"*, ComputerWeekly, February 2018.

[18] *"Can AI Become Our New Cybersecurity Sheriff?"* Forbes, February 2019.

[19] *"The Current Limitations and Future Potential of AI in Cybersecurity"*, Security Week, May 2018.

[20] *"AI for Cybersecurity is a Hot New Thing — And a Dangerous Gamble"*, MIT Technology Review, August 2018.

Table 3.1. Cybersecurity Threats: Conventional Approach vs AI-enabled Approach.

Cybersecurity threat(s)	Conventional approach	AI-enabled approach
Malware	Anti-virus, etc. uses signature-based detection to flag attacks Limitations: Covers known vulnerabilities	Pattern recognition and predictive analytics to thwart new attacks Advancement with AI: Can cover "zero day" exploits
Distributed Denial of Service (DDoS)	Analysts monitor network traffic to spot on-going DDoS attacks Limitations: Resource intensive, limited by human cognition, reactive	Algorithms auto-detect abnormal network resource allocation Advancement with AI: Efficient analyst resources, automated, faster response
IoT & Endpoints	Manual device-level security updates through the cloud Limitations: *Ad-hoc* security, ineffective at scale	Network-level behavior analytics and entity-anomaly detection Advancement with AI: Real-time security, effective at scale
Social Engineering	Education on digital hygiene and countering hackers' tactics Limitations: Prone to human error	Education, social biometrics, and user-anomaly detection Advancement with AI: Less prone to human error

Source: *"Old-School vs New-School: How Artificial Intelligence is Transforming Cybersecurity"*, CBInsights, July 2017.

context of the application, the "explainable" elements of AI are important, and human operators need to be able to understand what the system is recommending, and why.[21]

3.3.2 *Blockchain and Cybersecurity*

While blockchain as a technology is not as mature as AI, there are also emerging discussions on how blockchain could boost cybersecurity, by providing:

- **Data integrity:** Blockchains use a data structure called the Merkle tree, where the hashes of child nodes are combined together into the

[21] *"AI can Deliver 'Faster Better Cheaper' Cybersecurity"*, ZDNet, August 2018.

parent node's header and this continues iteratively till it reaches the root node. The hash of all the transactions in a block is stored in the Merkle tree and if a node wants to verify if any transaction is changed, the node will have to build the Merkle tree using all the transactions of the block, making it simple to validate or invalidate a transaction. The Merkle tree data structure helps to maintain data integrity in the blockchain;

- **Decentralised infrastructure:** In a blockchain network, nodes are decentralised, and in a large network, nodes are globally distributed. Such an architecture with no central point of control helps to mitigate against a single point of failure in the network;
- **Transparency:** All transactions on the blockchain are immutable, i.e. no one can attempt to manipulate, amend, or remove any of the data which has been stored, once it has been validated by the network. If the transaction was to be changed on the network, every other block in the system would also need to be amended, which raises the barriers to manipulating the data in the network.

Forbes suggests blockchain promising use cases of blockchain in cybersecurity could include decentralised storage solutions, IoT security, safer DNS, and private messaging.[22] DARPA is also exploring the application of blockchain in areas related to cybersecurity, such as economics-driven security models, and how centralisation may impact the cybersecurity posture of permissionless distributed consensus protocols.[23]

3.4 Convergence of AI, Blockchain, Augmented Reality (AR), and Virtual Reality (VR)

3.4.1 *AI and AR/VR*

The convergence of AR, VR, and AI is driven by recent developments such as AI capabilities that foster real-time image and speech recognition;

---

[22] *"4 Promising Use Case of Blockchain in Cybersecurity"*, Forbes, January 2019.

[23] *"RFI: Applications and Barriers to Consensus Protocols (ABC)"*, DARPA, November 2018.

increased availability and lower cost of local processing and storage; expanding network bandwidth to allow richer data streams; and the availability of AI in the cloud.[24]

When AI is applied to the development of VR and AR, it is anticipated that the convergence of these technologies would result in a more natural and intuitive immersive environment. For example, machine-learning powered advances in computer vision and spatial awareness will enable enhanced motion tracking, allowing designers to create experiences that users control with subtle, natural movements of their fingers and hands. Advances in natural language processing will enable intuitive voice commands and character interactions, making for even more immersive experiences.[25]

In retail, VR had been implemented to enhance shopping experience to let shoppers try out products that they are considering in a virtual environment before they make a purchase, such as trying on clothing, test drive a car, etc. With the addition of AI into the virtual retail space, it can enhance the VR experience to be more interactive. For instance, retail stores can introduce in-environment AI-powered virtual salespeople who can make suggestions, listen to customer feedback, and complete a sale. Retailers are able to learn about their customers' preferences and deliver a higher level of personalisation, making things convenient and efficient for the customers. The convergence of AI and VR not only benefits consumers, but also offers great possibilities for businesses for retailers.[26]

In tourism, players are integrating VR and AI to provide a pleasant and dynamic experience for travelers. Prospective travelers can use VR to tour locations they are interested in and the real-life environments replicated give them a visual idea of what to expect. Booking.com did a study and found that 80% of their customers prefer to acquire the information they want for their travel themselves, rather than assisted by a customer service officer. The addition of an AI-powered backend helps individuals complete their searches and bookings without the need for an

---

[24] *"AI Trends Weekly Brief: Convergence of AI with Augmented Reality and Virtual Reality"*, AI Trends, September 2017.

[25] *"AI-boosted VR/AR Could Transform Training"*, Booz Allen Hamilton.

[26] *"VR and AI: Two Technologies Set To Merge"*, VR Vision Group, July 2019.

intermediary, in aspects where decision-making is involved, making the entire process convenient and efficient.[27]

In healthcare, AI built into AR glasses will provide physicians with immediately accessible and maximally relevant information (parsed from the entirety of a patient's medical records and current research) to aid in accurate diagnoses and treatments, freeing doctors to engage in the more human-centric tasks of establishing trust, educating patients, and demonstrating empathy. An example will be the pilot between Microsoft and Philips to integrate and display rich 2D and 3D data in mixed reality, combined with gestures, eye-tracking, and voice control.[28]

3.4.2 *Blockchain and AR/VR*

AR and VR require extensive computing power for them to function seamlessly and blockchain is able to provide a decentralised network of users to share their spare processing power, thus enabling AR and VR applications to scale.[29]

The following examples illustrate the integration of blockchain technology into several various AR/VR industries:

- **Live entertainment:** Many of the lucrative, in-demand live events' tickets are highly priced. Through the integration of VR on live events, users can pay to access "near-live" experiences in a way that is more realistic than television and more affordable than attending in person. Services are emerging to offer the ability to transport somebody virtually to their favorite concert or sporting event simply by strapping on their headset, as well as integrated blockchain technology, primarily as a form of currency by which users can pay for these experiences. For instance, Ceek,[30] developed a platform using ERC20 Ethereum smart contract capabilities,[31] allowing users

---

[27] *"The Convergence of AI & VR — What You Can Expect"*, Data Driven Investor, August 2018.

[28] *"Exploring Industry-leading Solutions for HoloLens2"*, Microsoft.

[29] *"ADN Insights: 4 Technologies Adopting Blockchain Today"*, Medium, November 2019.

[30] *"Ceek VR"*, Ceek, 2018.

[31] *"4 New Platforms Combining VR and Blockchain"*, Investopedia, December 2017.

to vote for the acts they want to attend virtually and to transact securely on the blockchain, which provides an immutable record of exchanges;

- **Virtual eCommerce:** According to Google, roughly 50% of consumers look for videos about a product online before they order it or visit a store to purchase the item. Online retailers, especially in the fashion industry, are exploring to utilise the VR experience to give their customers a greater sense of what an item looks like without having to travel to a physical location. The blockchain technology has emerged as a reliable, interoperable means of establishing and storing copyrights for these digital creations. As more industries and customers come to embrace VR, these copyrights will become increasingly important to protect;
- **Digital Advertising:** Advertising and the modern gaming landscape are inextricably linked. An estimated 10–30% of revenues for social games are the result of advertising and generating US$39.8 billion in 2017. In fact, 78% of the 50 highest-grossing gaming apps in the US featured advertisements in 2017, an increase from 45% in 2016.[32] As VR gaming gains traction, similar advertising models are likely to arise and tracking the effectiveness of advertisement campaigns in virtual worlds is necessary to gauge how well advertising dollars are being spent. Blockchain-linked coins have been developed that allow users to interact with advertisements as they explore virtual worlds, and the effectiveness of these advertisements are measured through, among other metrics, the tracking of eye movements to measure the attention each advertisement commands. Compensating users with coins for interacting with these advertisements and logging information about their interactions on a blockchain ledger are ways that blockchain technology is going to impact the advertising landscape in the world of VR. GazeCoin[33] is a patent-registered blockchain platform measured by gaze control/eye tracking and uses a custom engine to track a VR viewer's eye movements, which can determine

[32] *"Mobile Game Developers Turn to "Rewarded Ads""*, Business Insider, August 2017.
[33] *"Gaze Coin"*, GazeCoin, 2019.

exactly how much attention they're paying to sponsored content, rewarding them and advertisers proportionately;

- **VR Gaming:** It is one of the most obvious and widespread application for VR/AR technology. Among its prominent examples are Pokémon Go, Beat Saber, and Robo Recall. Blockchain technology is being used in ensuring security when users buy and sell online gaming items.[34] Decentraland, a virtual world accessible through any normal VR headset, is developed on the Ethereum blockchain. It allows players to use cryptocurrency to record their irrefutable ownership over parcels of land onto it. A player's virtual land can be developed (literally) with houses, businesses, or other services and monetised accordingly.[35]

3.5 Convergence of Blockchain and Autonomous Robotics

Autonomous robots such as drones and autonomous vehicles (AVs) are revolutionising many industrial applications, from targeted material delivery to precision farming. However, one of the main obstacles to the large-scale deployment of robots for commercial applications is security, which covers fundamental aspects such as data confidentiality, data integrity, entity authentication, and data origin authentication. This is due to the complex and heterogeneous characteristics of robotic swarm systems, e.g. robot autonomy, decentralised control, collective emergent behavior, etc. Blockchain technology demonstrates that by combining peer-to-peer networks with cryptographic algorithms a group of agents can reach an agreement, and creates an immutable record without the need for a controlling authority. The combination of blockchain with other distributed systems, such as robotic swarm systems, can provide a suitable framework with capabilities to make robotic swarm operations more secure, autonomous, and flexible.[36]

The implementation of blockchain technology across a wide array of industries has altered the way many key decision-makers approach

---

[34] *"How Blockchain Will Revolutionize VR/AR Technology"*, Xsolus Inc, February 2019.

[35] *"Designing and Building Blockchain Games"*, Decentraland, 2019.

[36] *"The Blockchain: A New Framework for Robotic Swarm Systems"*, MIT, June 2017.

recognising and exchanging value. Industry-specific applications built on top of blockchain technology have the capacity to create new ecosystems to allow secure and immutable data exchange. A decentralised network can be used as an ecosystem of connected component parts, which can not only connect cars to cars or drones to drones, but can also be extended to link any and all AVs including cars, trucks, rovers, and drones, along with the vital infrastructure required.[37]

By removing the middle layer like administrators approving transactions, it becomes necessary for vehicles themselves to interact with charging stations and other vital infrastructure. One such application of this would be if several organisations have their own separate fleets of ride-hailing vehicles. Despite this being a traditionally "siloed" system, they can use the infrastructure that the network provides without interfering with each other. This is beneficial for the vehicle providers, as they no longer need to develop their own infrastructure for the fleet. By joining the ecosystem and using the services that already exist within, they can reach the wider market more easily.

In the automotive industry, there is a need to share driving data and driving patterns around the world, to produce safe AVs. The Mobility Open Blockchain Initiative (MOBI), a global consortium backed by vehicle manufacturers such as BMW, GM, Renault, and Ford, seeks to harmonise the development of distributed ledger technology (DLT) across the "smart mobility" industry.[38] Ocean Protocol, being part of the MOBI consortium, is a decentralised data exchange protocol to unlock data for AI. Through blockchain technology and smart contracts, Ocean Protocol connects data providers and consumers, allowing data to be shared while guaranteeing traceability, transparency, and trust for all stakeholders involved. It allows data owners to give value to and have control over their data assets without being locked-in to any single marketplace. The integration of decentralised blockchain technology, a data sharing framework, and an ecosystem for data and related services will accelerate the development of connected cars and autonomous mobility solutions in this industry.[39]

---

[37] *"The Link Between Autonomous Vehicles and Blockchain"*, Forbes, October 2018.

[38] *"GM, BMW Back Blockchain Data Sharing For Self-Driving Cars"*, Coindesk, April 2019.

[39] *"IBM Hosts First APAC MOBI Colloquium to Promote Standards and Accelerate Adoption of Blockchain in Human Mobility"*, PR Newswire, April 2019.

3.6 Convergence of AI, Blockchain, and 3D Printing

Industries like aerospace, pharmaceuticals, and energy are amongst the first to receive the benefits of technological convergence of emerging technologies such as AI, blockchain, and 3D printing.

3.6.1 *Aerospace*

The convergence of 3D printing and blockchain enables the conversion of bits to atoms at the point of use and time of need, thus creating a smart distributed digital supply chain. This convergence drives the non-value added process out of supply changes such as packaging, shipping, warehousing, inventory management, customs brokerage fees, etc. This method significantly reduces overhead costs and increases the efficiency of traditional manufacturing processes.

Moog Inc, a precision actuation company with additive manufacturing capability, is leveraging on technology convergence in the aerospace manufacturing vertical. Additive manufacturing involves using Computer Aided Design (CAD) and 3D printing technologies to produce aircraft parts in precise geometric shapes.[40] Despite these improvements, additive manufacturing faces challenges like:

- **Technology:** Different design principles and stress data for each different additive manufacturing technology;
- **Data management:** Future geographical and/or organisational separation of the design and production organisations requires a secure transfer of approved design data (i.e. build file, material specifications);
- **Business:** Intellectual property protection for design and printing data.

To address these challenges, Moog has developed "VeriPart", a technology solution that converges blockchain technology with the 3D printing and additive manufacturing. This hybrid solution is a blockchain-enabled

---

[40] *"Blockchain and the Need for Tech Convergence: Three Industry Case Studies"*, Frost & Sullivan, January 2019.

supply chain that stores the history of the design-manufacture-use cycle, secures the transportation of data, facilitates digital rights management/ licensable transactions, and provides a proof of authenticity for printed goods and assemblies.

Moog and ST Aerospace Ltd. announced their collaboration to explore and develop capabilities for a smart digital supply chain that will power Industry 4.0 for the global aerospace sector. The collaboration aims to develop additive manufacturing technology with digital transaction capability to bring about greater efficiency and security in aftermarket services. The result will optimise supply chain improvements within military and commercial aerospace markets, while meeting trade compliance regulations.[41]

3.6.2 *Pharmaceutical*

In the pharmaceutical industry, companies are leveraging on this convergence to handle the design, production, and distribution process of pharmaceutical products in a more open and integrated supply chain.

With AI, pharmaceutical companies are able to develop algorithms that can absorb highly complex data sets and apply biomechanical principles to accurately predict the success of a drug prior to its development, saving huge amounts of time and money from clinical trials.

3D printing technology represents the next stage of automated manufacturing. Traditionally, drug manufacturing has been a fragmented process that usually results in overproduction or lack of accurate dosing. Now with the help of 3D printers, pharmaceutical companies can develop personalised drugs with increasing precision and efficiency, saving both time and money.

Nonetheless, blockchain technology is the final component, which provides counterfeit detection and secure distribution. Blockchains provide access to an open distributed ledger for manufacturers, transporters, hospital, pharmacies, and patients to keep track of a drug's location at all

[41] *"Moog and ST Aerospace to Collaborate on Industry's First: Blockchain and 3D Printing-enabled Total Digital Transaction"*, ST Engineering, February 2018.

times. Blockchains are also immutable, preventing malicious actors from tampering with the records in order to cover up incidents of theft.

Technology convergences are an essential part of how AI, blockchain, and 3D printing will reach their full transformative potential. However, for industries to achieve mass scale adoption, there are scalability challenges to be considered. For instance, we need the system to provide automatic updates of any changes made to the physical asset back to the blockchain platform, in order to maintain trust in the monetary value of a tokenised real-world asset. In addition, IoT sensors in a manufacturing supply chain need to converge with the AI algorithms to provide applicable adjustments back to the supply chain. In order to overcome scalability challenges, AI, blockchain, and 3D printing must accentuate each other's strengths and compensate for each other's weaknesses. Only then, through the adoption of hybrid applications that enhance design, production, and distribution processes will we witness exponential growth in industries like aerospace, pharmaceuticals, clean energy, and many more.

3.7 Convergence of Quantum Computing, AI, and Blockchain

3.7.1 *Quantum Computing and Blockchain*

Section 2.4.4.7 discusses the threat posed by quantum computing to blockchain, and how the application of quantum technologies (e.g. quantum random number generators, quantum key distribution, etc) in blockchains are a potential means to mitigate this. MIT summarises this eloquently: "If quantum computers break blockchains, quantum blockchains could be the defense."[42]

3.7.2 *Quantum Computing and AI*

Section 2.3.2.6 discusses the emergence of quantum machine learning, a new field that has emerged where quantum versions of machine learning

---

[42] "*If Quantum Computers Break Blockchains, Quantum Blockchains Could Be the Defense*", MIT Technology Review, May 2018.

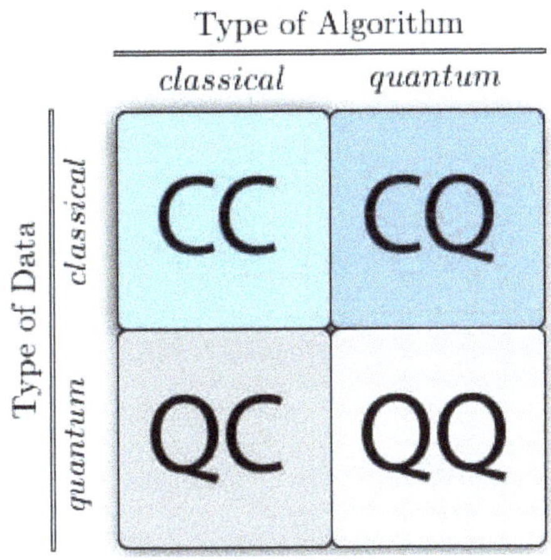

Figure 3.5. Four Approaches to Machine Learning.
Source: *"How Quantum Computing and Machine Learning Work Together"*, Hackernoon, June 2018.

algorithms are developed, and where classical machine learning algorithms are used to analyse quantum systems.[43] The matrix in Figure 3.5 describes the four approaches to machine learning, as a result of this intersection.

An IBM/MIT study provides early demonstration of how quantum computing can bolster machine learning.[44] Industry examples include the Google Quantum AI initiative, which looks into advancing quantum computing by developing quantum processors and novel quantum algorithms; the lab also unveiled a quantum AI chip in March 2018.[45] Chipset players such as Qualcomm have also indicated interest in quantum AI chips.[46]

On the flipside, AI can also offer a means to advance quantum computing, as indicated by an Intel study.[47]

---

[43] *"Quantum Machine Learning: An Overview"*, KDNuggets, January 2018.
[44] *"Finally, Proof that Quantum Computing Can Boost Machine Learning"*, SingularityHub, March 2019.
[45] *"Google Unveils World's Most Powerful Quantum AI"*, AIBusiness, March 2018.
[46] *"Qualcomm Aims for Quantum AI Chips"*, NextBigFuture, April 2019.
[47] *"Intel Offers AI Breakthrough in Quantum Computing"*, ZDNet, March 2019.

Chapter 4

The Impact and Implications of AI, Data and Blockchain

4.1 Introduction

The emergence of AI, data and blockchain technologies and the convergence of technologies have various impacts and implications at country, enterprise, and societal levels. Countries and enterprises recognise the economic potential and competitive advantages of such technologies, hence the growing investments in AI and blockchain. The expectation is that these innovative technologies would enable countries to capture economic growth and benefits whilst organisations would enjoy improvements in efficiency and productivity, simultaneously realising product innovation. Finally, beyond impacting countries and enterprises, these technologies also have broader social implications.

4.2 Country-Level Implications

4.2.1 *Artificial Intelligence*

A number of global studies performed by consulting firms such as Accenture, McKinsey, and PricewaterhouseCoopers (PwC) emphasised that AI will have a significant economic impact (see Figure 4.1).

Having identified the economic potential of AI, a number of countries are actively investing in AI with the launch of national AI strategies. These strategies take a coordinated approach in harmonising government

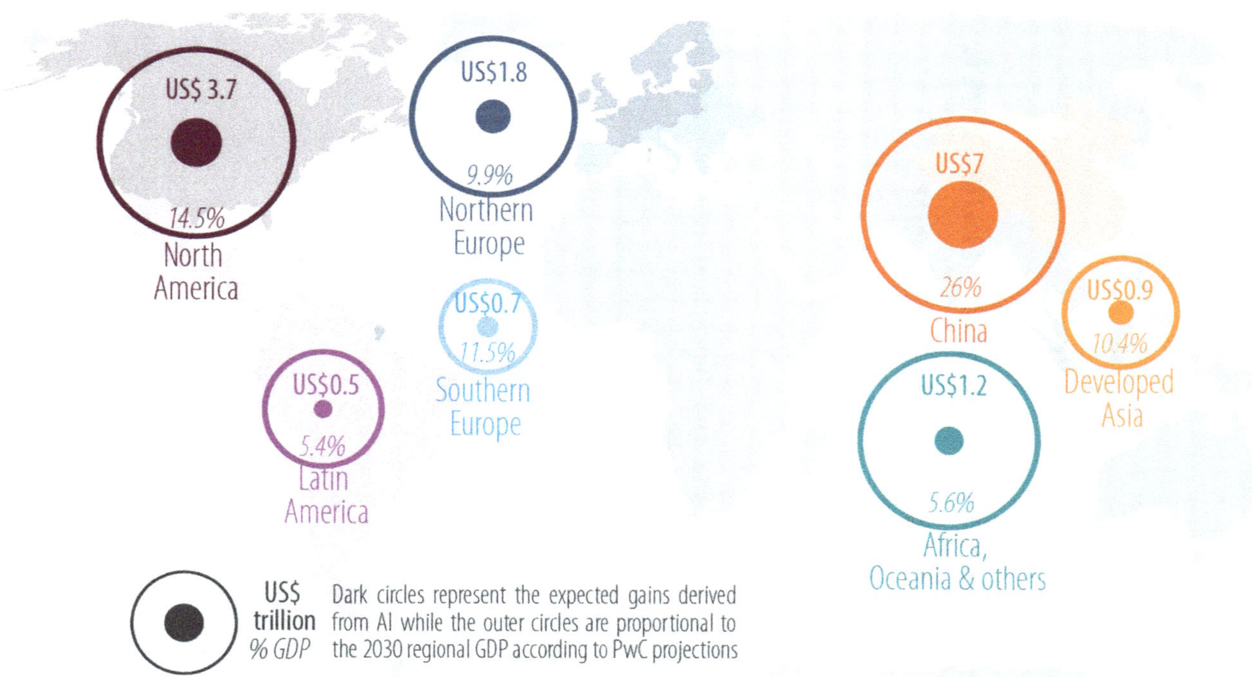

Figure 4.1. Expected Gains from AI in the Different Regions of the World by 2030.

Source: *"Economic Impacts of Artificial Intelligence"*, European Parliamentary Research Service, 2019.

policies with a clear objective of maximising the potential benefits and minimising the potential costs of AI for the economy and society.[1] For example, Australia has allocated approximately US$22 million of its federal budget over four years to fund AI and machine learning,[2] while investments by Canada and Singapore are over US$92 million; Taiwan, France, UK, and South Korea each invested over US$1 billion. Furthermore, nine countries, such as China, India, Japan, Sweden, and Germany have released guiding documents on AI. Figure 4.2 summarises the current landscape of AI strategies globally.

The focus and priority areas of the nations and regions can be categorised into eight areas, that are not mutually exclusive — scientific research, AI talent development, skills and future of work, industrialisation of AI technologies, ethical AI standards, data and digital infrastructure, AI in the government, inclusion, and social well-being. The industrialisation of AI technologies is a top priority in most nation strategies, followed by scientific research. AI talent development and ethical AI standards are also priority areas, while inclusion and social well-being, future of work, and AI in the government received the least attention.

4.2.1.1 *Scientific Research*

The plans to launch new research centers or programmes or increase funding in AI research fall into this category. It is one of the most consistently emphasised areas, with 15 out of 17 countries and regions (except for Italy and UAE) included in the national AI strategies, all of which assign quite great emphasis. About half of them identify research in AI as (one of) a top priority to generate top-tier research and innovation to attract, retain, and develop talent; the countries include Canada, India, Mexico, Singapore, South Korea, and Sweden.

---

[1] *"Building an AI World: Report on National and Regional AI Strategies"*, Tim Dutton, Brent Barron, & Gaga Boskovic, CIFAR, December 2018.

[2] *"Government Should Lead AI Certification: Finkel"*, Georgia Clark, May 2018.

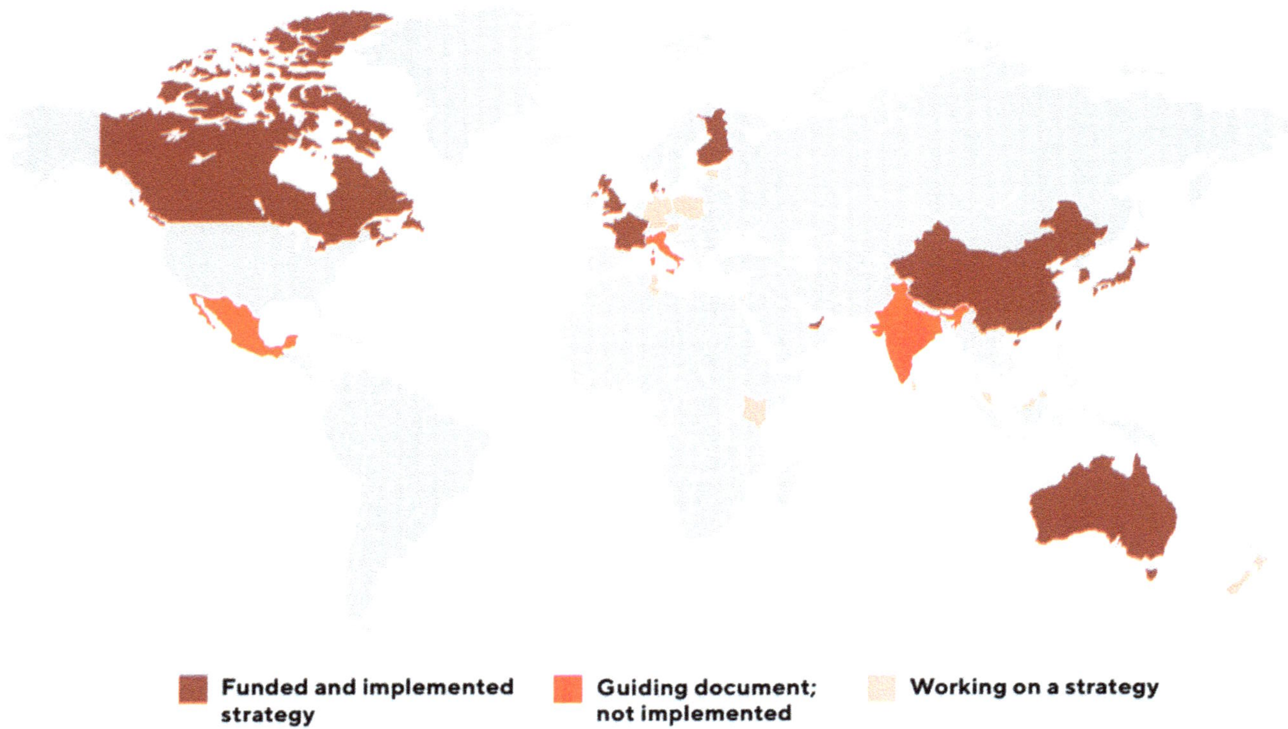

Figure 4.2. AI Strategy Landscape.

Source: *"Building an AI World: Report on National and Regional AI Strategies"*, Tim Dutton, Brent Barron, and Gaga Boskovic, CIFAR, December 2018.

4.2.1.2 *AI Talent Development*

All 17 countries and regions under evaluation cited AI talent as one of the priority areas in their national strategies. Investing in AI talent is important for the advancement of AI and talents are in great demand. In fact, according to an IBM report, an estimated 120 million workers worldwide will need to be retrained due to the development in AI and automation within the next three years.[3] Of all the countries, France places the greatest emphasis on AI talent, and it aims to double trained AI practitioners in five years.

4.2.1.3 *Skills and Future of Work*

About half of the strategies incorporate initiatives to help students and overall workforce develop skills for the future of work, among which Denmark and Mexico assign higher priority to this area. For instance, Denmark invests in education in STEM (science, technology, engineering, and mathematics) subjects and encourages understanding of emerging technologies in elementary schools. Mexico and Singapore are promoting AI learning beyond STEM students in public and private universities. Finland will teach AI literacy through massive open online courses to raise the AI awareness and capability of its people.

4.2.1.4 *Industrialisation of AI Technologies*

Industrial strategy refers to initiatives and programmes to encourage private-sector adoption of AI technologies. A wide range of countries identify industrialisation as the key focus, such as Australia, China, Finland, Japan, Singapore, and UK. Australia is developing a technology roadmap and standards framework to identify global opportunities and guide future AI investments, Japan provides support for start-ups, and Singapore is developing an AI ecosystem.

---

[3] *"The Enterprise Guide to Closing the Skills Gap"*, IBM Institute for Business Value, September 2019.

4.2.1.5 *Ethical AI Standards*

Standards or regulations for the ethical use and development of AI are accounted for in most strategies, but usually with slighter emphasis. Italy and Sweden are examples of the nations that place ethics on the top priority list. An AI research center in Italy leads the debate on ethics and experts and citizens are involved in the regulation of AI. China aims to develop a world-leading AI standard setting and code of ethics, and establish an explainable and accountable AI system.

4.2.1.6 *Data and Digital Infrastructure*

Similar to ethics, most national strategies mention this focus area, but with less priority in general. Italy, however, lists it as the second most important aspect. It plans to launch a national AI platform to support annotation of data. UK aims to provide legal certainty over data usage and sharing, and improve its digital infrastructure.

4.2.1.7 *AI in the Government*

AI in government refers to pilot programmes that use AI to improve government efficiency, service delivery, and public administration less commonly considered in national strategies, but countries like Italy and UAE focus almost exclusively in this area. The National Competence Centre in Italy facilitates adoption of AI solutions in public sector and the overall strategy of UAE is to improve the efficiency and effectiveness of its government.

4.2.1.8 *Inclusion and Social Well-Being*

For India, inclusion and social well-being is a key priority given India's overarching goal to leverage AI for inclusion. Germany is promoting diversity in AI to strengthen social partnerships and include all actors in consultation.

4.2.2 *Blockchain*

There is an observable shift from cryptocurrencies to blockchain. Some commonly cited challenges impeding the adoption of blockchain technology include the lack of regulations and standards, privacy, digital identity, and data protection.[4] To promote the technology and related markets, policymakers are working on provide guiding principles related to data integrity and protection of users' and citizens' rights, as well as to attract investors, increasing the market efficiency that will help businesses grow.

4.2.2.1 *Legal and Regulatory Network*

The decentralised and distributed nature of blockchain, notably its ability to cross jurisdictional boundaries, can pose challenges for regulators to identify the appropriate governing set of rules to decide upon the applicable or relevant jurisdiction for enforcement. However, nations worldwide are paying attention to emerging blockchain technology and some initiatives are made towards a more mature regulatory environment to govern blockchain companies. An increasing number of countries are looking into setting up blockchain registries. For example, France recognised companies' blockchain technology registry in cash vouchers as early as 2016, and has established an innovative legal framework to regulate Initial Coin Offerings (ICOs) and digital assets services providers.[5] In China, more than 500 blockchain projects are registered with the Cyberspace Administration of China[6] and the country has passed a new cryptography law that will take effect on 1 January 2020 to regulate how the technology will be used by the government, businesses, and citizens.[7]

---

[4] *"Legal and Regulatory Framework of Blockchains and Smart Contracts"*, European Union Blockchain Observatory & Forum, 27 September 2019.

[5] *"Blockchain & Cryptocurrency Regulation 2020 | France"*, Global Legal Insights, 23 October 2019.

[6] *"From Banking Giants to Tech Darlings, China Reveals Over 500 Enterprise Blockchain Projects"*, David Pan, CoinDesk, 28 October 2019.

[7] *"China Passes New Cryptography Law"*, Anthony Spadafora, 29 October 2019.

Recognising blockchain registries may be the first steps towards more comprehensive regulatory functions of the government and these are encouraging developments for the blockchain-enabled market.

4.2.2.2 *Personal Data Protection*

Blockchain technology has implications on the storage of personal data, and regulators around the world that are involved in personal data protection are looking into this area. Examples of countries with data protection laws include Singapore's Personal Data Protection Act and the European Union's General Data Protection Regulations.[8] Some areas being taken into consideration by regulators in examining blockchain in the context of data protection include: identification and obligations of data controllers and processors, anonymisation of personal data as cryptography techniques adopted in cryptocurrencies may not fully conceal users' identities, and the exercise of some data subject rights such as rectification or removal, which could pose challenges in the context of blockchain.[9]

4.2.2.3 *Blockchain for Government and Public Services*

Blockchain is also being tested in government and public services to enhance government operational efficiency. Examples of use cases with the potential for government agencies to adopt blockchain, include education, tax fraud detection, health data protection, and government waste mitigation. In addition, by getting involved in the technology, governments can gain a better understanding of the technology and thus improve government's role as regulatory bodies. Table 4.1 tabulates examples of governmental initiatives worldwide in the application of blockchain.

---

[8] *"Blockchain & Cryptocurrency Regulation 2019, First Edition"*, Global Legal Insights, Global Legal Group Ltd, London, August 2018.

[9] *"Blockchain and the GDPR"*, European Union Blockchain Observatory & Forum, October 2018.

Table 4.1. Examples of Blockchain in Governments.

Use case	Countries
Digital currency/payments	Canada, Singapore, United Arab Emirates, Saudi Arabia
Land rights	United States, Brazil, Sweden
Voting in elections	United States, Australia, Japan, South Korea
Shareholder proxies	United Arab Emirates
Identity management	Switzerland, Estonia, United Arab Emirates, Singapore
Healthcare	United States, Estonia
Defence/security	United States

Source: *"Will Blockchain Transform the Public Sector?"* Jason Killmeyer, Mark White, and Bruce Chew, Deloitte University Press, September 2017.

Blockchain is also being tried out on voting systems to explore reduction in electoral fraud and mitigation of mistrust on current political process and voting mechanisms. Companies like Voatz, Votem, and Smartmatic-Cybernetica are developing blockchain technology to manage identification of voters and improve the integrity of voting results.[10] The Democracy Earth Foundation brought up the idea of "liquid democracy" where people can delegate their votes on specific issues to proxies they personally know and trust, promoting a system of representative and direct democracy.[11]

In addition, OS City, a software company based in San Pedro, Mexico, focuses on improving transparency and accountability of government operations in cities across Latin America. OS City incorporated blockchain into its platforms and deploys a range of blockchain-based solutions to support the administration of city government operations across Latin America.[12]

---

[10] *"Blockchain Applications: Election Voting"*, Denise Tambanis, Blockchain Philanthropy Foundation, February 2019.

[11] *"Democracy is Getting A Reboot on the Blockchain"*, Adele Peters, FastCompany, October 2016.

[12] *"Blockchain for Social Impart 2019"*, Center for Social Innovation, Stanford Graduate School of Business, September 2019.

4.3 Enterprise-Level Implications

4.3.1 *Artificial Intelligence*

The innovative changes in AI and blockchain technologies will affect companies in many ways as they bring both unprecedented opportunities and new challenges. Such technologies could raise efficiency, reduce manpower costs, and enable companies to realise product innovation to enhance their customer offerings.

4.3.1.1 *Enterprise Adoption of AI*

Enterprise adoption of AI grew 270% over the past four years and tripled in the past year, rising from 25% in 2018 to 37% in 2019, according to the Gartner, Inc. 2019 CIO Survey.[13] AI capabilities have matured significantly and enterprises are more willing to implement the technology, thus greatly pushing the adoption of AI for enterprises. About 49% of enterprises are already changing their business models to integrate and adopt new technological solutions throughout their internal processes and supply chains. Based on Gartner's AI business value forecast projections, the largest type of AI by business value-add is decision support/augmentation (44% by 2030) followed by agents (24% by 2030), decision automation (19% by 2030), and smart products (13% by 2030).[14]

4.3.1.2 *Product Innovation*

Emerging technologies often provide alternative perspectives or solutions to the existing bottleneck in the business environment, especially for the sectors most relevant to the technologies. Industry adoption of AI has expanded from mainly in large technology firms to a wider spectrum of companies, and statistics show that AI has a large potential that it may add around 16% or US$13 trillion to global output by 2030. Increasingly,

---

[13] *"Gartner Survey Shows 37 Percent of Organizations have Implemented AI in Some Form"*, Gartner, January 2019.

[14] *"Gartner Says AI Augmentation will Create $2.9 Trillion of Business Value in 2021"*, Gartner, August 2019.

more and more companies are looking into providing innovative products, services, and solutions using AI.

4.3.1.2.1 Customer Service

The development in AI will result in innovative changes in customer service and an enhanced customer service experience. The improvement in speech recognition, natural language processing, activity recognition in computer vision, and algorithm will improve the performance of the existing AI chatbot. Furthermore, we may anticipate the rise of the next generation of AI assistants referred to as AI avatars, embodied interactive virtual AI assistants that employ AI and augmented reality (AR) technologies. TwentyBN, a Canadian startup, created the world's first context-aware digital companion named Millie in December 2018,[15] aiming to offer all kinds of personal care suggestions by observing and understanding what customers say and what they do. Many other AI avatars have been launched and used since then. There are numerous applications across industries, from promoting shopping experience in retail and e-commerce to increasing learning efficiency in education and learning. Some people even argue that such avatars will help build an "avatar layer" that connects businesses to customers in entirely new ways and reshapes the relationship between companies and consumers.[16]

4.3.1.2.2 Product Development and Hyper-personalisation

With available abundant data and AI algorithms, businesses are moving towards sophisticated data-driven marketing strategies to develop products and target customers with products that interest them and cater to their specific needs, which is also referred to as hyper-personalisation. It would create hyper-personalised experiences for customers, simplify the purchase-decision process, and make sales more efficient and satisfied. An Accenture research found that 49% of the consumers do not mind having

[15] *"Meet Millie, the First Context-Aware A.I."*, Twenty Billion Neurons, December 2018.
[16] *"The Rise of a New Generation of AI Avatars"*, Aaron Frank, January 2019.

their buying behaviours tracked if it would result in relevant offers.[17] Quite a few organisations are investing in this realm. For example, using the results of a DNA test is generating opportunities for businesses like LifeDNA and Equinox as they offer highly personalised wellness products and services such as diet, fitness programmes, supplements, and skincare kits that are tailored to their genetic needs.[18]

4.3.2 *Blockchain*

According to a recent survey done by Deloitte, blockchain technology had been deemed as a critical priority by the organisations of 53% of respondents in 2019, 10% higher than that of previous year, and the percentage of respondents that see compelling use cases for blockchain had increased from 74% in 2018 to 83% in 2019.[19] Respondents see the benefits of blockchain applicable across business models, value chains innovation, greater security risk, and greater speed compared to existing systems.

Blockchain research and solutions have been active in financial industries for a few years. For instance, a handful of financial companies, including Barclays, Credit Suisse, and Goldman Sachs, started the R3 consortium to prove enterprise blockchain platform as early as 2015. Companies like MasterCard applied for a blockchain-based patent in 2016. In the automobile sector, several manufacturers are considering blockchain in response to the trending innovation of technologies that will change the ride sharing and human–vehicle interactions. Toyota works on a blockchain-based decentralised exchange of autonomous vehicle driving data transaction and car sharing platform, and Volkswagen is exploring the telematics tracking using blockchain for data integrity and transparency.[20]

---

[17] *"Hyper-personalisation: The Evolution of Customer Engagement"*, Nina Conseil, MarketingTech, September 2017.

[18] *"World's First Hyper-Personalized Line of Supplements and Skincare Kits Tailored to Customers' DNA Using a Free DNA Test"*, PR Newswire, February 2018.

[19] *"Deloitte's 2019 Global Blockchain Survey: Blockchain Gets Down to Business"*, Deloitte Insights, 2019.

[20] *"Blockchain in Enterprise: How Companies are Using Blockchain Today"*, Ashley Lannquist, Blockchain at Berkeley, January 2018.

Walmart and nine other retail and food companies such as Nestlé and Unilever have been collaborating with IBM on a blockchain-based initiative to track food globally through the supply chain since 2016 and began trails in 2017.[21] In Asia, the three Internet giants in China, Baidu, Alibaba, and Tencent, entered the realm of blockchain at an early phase and all of them have started initiatives to become blockchain service providers.

4.4 Societal-Level Implications

With the rapid development of AI and blockchain technologies, the broader impact on social aspects is as important as that on the national and enterprise or industrial applications.

4.4.1 *Artificial Intelligence*

4.4.1.1 *Jobs and Skills*

Increased operational efficiency brought on by AI is desirable for enterprises due to its potential to reduce manpower costs and increase performance as well as profits. However, it brings issues to broader social impact due to implications on jobs and the challenges posted on employees. Based on an *MIT Technology Review* study, the adoption of AI will alter work for blue-collar workers and in fact disrupt the future work lives of white-collar workers the most.[22]

Without a skilled workforce, the benefits to both nations and businesses will be very limited. Skills development to cater for the growing usage of technologies and emergence of digital economies interest not only the human resource department now, but a broader range of functions within an organisation. A study by Cisco and Oxford Economics on the impact of AI on workers in six South-east Asian economies found that Singapore faces the biggest skills challenge as the majority of new jobs created are in

---

[21] "*Walmart, IBM Blockchain Initiative Aims to Track Global Food Supply Chain*", Molly Jane Zuckerman, CoinTelegraph, June 2018.

[22] "*AI Will Disrupt White-collar Workers the Most, Predicts a New Report*", MIT Technology Review, November 2019.

highly-skilled professional and managerial roles.[23] A report on the talent shortage's influence on employers released in 2018 shows that nearly half of the organisations are unable to source for the skills they need due to mismatch in education and experience and lack of applicants.[24] Worse still, the rate at which skills learned become less valuable or even irrelevant is getting faster.[25] The negative impacts on workforce and skills cannot be neglected and addressing this issue requires efforts from the government, industries, educators, and individuals.

4.4.1.2 *Bias in AI*

One of the concerns against massive adoption of AI is transparency, also referred as the "black-box" problem, where it is unclear, or unexplainable, how the algorithms derive the results. The development in explainable AI has yet to be satisfactorily compared to the escalating need. To many, computer decisions can only be fully entrusted when there is clarity and transparency as to how it arrives at the conclusions and recommendations. However, today, there are examples of algorithms and/or training data being biased, resulting in biases in recommendations or results achieved. These tend to impact the minority, in areas such as race, gender, and socio-economic status.

Results have shown that facial recognition has greater difficulty differentiating between men and women with darker skin tone. A woman with dark skin is much more likely to be mistaken for a man.[26] Given the dominance of males in AI roles worldwide (about four in five programmers are male according to a study done by the World Economic Forum), AI programmes are being encoded with perspectives that are intrinsically not representative of the societies they serve, creating the potential for gender

---

[23] *"The Impact of AI on Workers in ASEAN's Six Largest Economies"*, Cisco and Oxford Economics, September 2018.

[24] *"2018 Talent Shortage Survey: Solving the Talent Shortage — Build, Buy, Borrow and Bridge"*, ManpowerGroup, 2018.

[25] *"Skill, Re-skill and Re-skill Again: How to Keep Up with the Future of Work"*, Kasriel Stephane, World Economic Forum, July 2017.

[26] *"Gender Shades: Intersectional Accuracy Disparities in Commercial Gender Classification"*, Joy Buolamwini and Timnit Gebru, 2018.

biases.[27] With this regard, ethical evaluations and algorithm audits can be considered in order to avoid the bias and boost transparency in the results generated by AI.

4.4.1.3 *Undermining of Trust*

As machine learning and reinforcement learning techniques are increasingly more advanced, especially with the significant improvements in generative adversarial networks (GANs), the content generated by AI can be highly realistic. Although there are many beneficial applications such as grammar correction and code autocompletion, the inability to detect machine-generated content may raise concerns about trust issues. In Feb 2019, an AI lab named OpenAI generated a language model that is so good at generating fake news that the organisation decided not to release it, and researchers of the model find that readers on average believed the outputs to be genuine news articles nearly as often as the *New York Times* ones.[28] This "fake news 2.0" that is personalised, optimised, and even harder to stop has already proved to be impactful in generating fake news by foreign operatives during presidential campaigns in US on social-media platforms.[29] What is worse, the development in speech recognition and analysis makes possible the mimicking of human voice.[30] Therefore, the undermining of trust is another social aspect to be cautioned in the development of AI.

4.4.1.4 *Liability in Automated Systems*

The liability of algorithms that perform unexpectedly is another implication of AI. When people suffer loss or experience system failures in an automated process even in highly automated systems where humans have

---

[27] *"Global Gender Gap Report 2018"*, World Economic Forum, 2018.

[28] *"OpenAI Has Released the Largest Version Yet of Its Fake-news-spewing AI"*, Karen Hao, August 2019.

[29] *"Fake News 2.0: Personalized, Optimized, and Even Harder to Stop"*, MIT Technology Review, March 2019.

[30] *"Fraudsters Used AI to Mimic CEO's Voice in Unusual Cybercrime Case"*, Catherine Stupp, August 2019.

limited control over its behaviour, the nearest human often gets the blame.[31] For instance, when a self-driving Uber struck and killed a pedestrian in 2018, Uber was subsequently exonerated of criminal liability, but the safety driver was faulted. When Air France flight 447 crashed into the Atlantic Ocean in 2009, subsequent investigation revealed the cause to be a mix of poor systems design and insufficient pilot training. However, the public quickly latched onto a narrative that placed the sole blame on the pilots, even though significant research factors demonstrate that humans have always been relatively inept at leaping into emergency situations at the last minute with a level head and clear mind.

This is an important social implication that regulators are examining, and there could potentially be a need for legal and regulatory frameworks to address the fair distribution of liability in automated systems.

4.4.2 *Blockchain*

4.4.2.1 *Financial Inclusion*

According to the World Bank, as of 2017, there are still about 1.7 billion of the world's adults who are unbanked — without an account at a financial institution or through a mobile financial service provider — and the majority of the unbanked population resides in the developing economies.[32] Financial inclusion has also been identified as an enabler for seven of the United Nations' 17 Sustainable Development Goals (SDGs). In short, financial inclusion plays an important role in various social aspects, such as eliminating poverty, creating jobs, improving gender equality or good health, and easing the refugee crisis,[33] and blockchain technology can be a useful tool in achieving financial inclusion.

On one hand, blockchain can lower the cost of transactions that occur in payments and money transfers, especially in cross-border cases. For

[31] *"When Algorithms Mess Up, the Nearest Human Gets the Blame"*, MIT Technology Review, May 2019.

[32] *"The Global Findex Database 2017"*, World Bank, 2017.

[33] *"Achieving the Sustainable Development Goals — The Role of Financial Inclusion"*, Leora Klapper, Mayada El-Zoghbi, and Jake Hess, Consultative Group to Assist the Poor (CGAP), April 2016.

example, Sentinel Chain adopts blockchain to enable the use of livestock as collaterals and brings ordinary financial services such as banking, loans, and insurance to unbanked people such as farmers in Myanmar[34]; Wala, a fintech company that operates in Uganda, Zimbabwe, and South Africa, has built a mobile platform to allow its users to store and transfer funds securely quickly using blockchain.[35]

On the other hand, blockchain can provide platforms and marketplaces that are borderless, distributed, and have better outreach and transparency so that users can gain access to financial services without worrying too much about leakage of personal identity and privacy. For example, a blockchain startup named UBDI, which stands for "Universal Basic Data Income", offers a blockchain-based platform that allows individuals to get compensated for sharing anonymous and aggregated insights from their data, which will be stored in a secure, encrypted, and decentralised data vault with selected access.[36] This may provide a new perspective to the poor or the companies that are working towards financial inclusion. Blockchain has other advantages that can help boost financial inclusion such as its usage in records and verification.

4.4.2.2 *Emerging Economies*

Many first adoptions and trails of blockchain start with the financial service industry, and emerging markets may serve as an ideal place where blockchain-based financial solutions can be adopted and tested due to the underserved populations, lower bank penetration, and higher banking risks, especially when increasing number of people are using mobile phones that pave the way for digital finance. Also, for the past few years, many emerging economies have witnessed a decreasing

---

[34] *"Government Partners with Fintech Firms to Enable Use of Livestock as Collateral"*, Thiha Ko Ko, Myanmar Times, May 2018.

[35] *"Blockchain for Social Impact"*, Center for Social Innovation, Stanford Graduate School of Business, September 2019.

[36] *"UBDI Raises About $1 Million for a blockchain-powered Platform that Empowers Consumers to Monetize Insights from Personal Data, Creating a Universal Basic Data Income"*, TechStartups Team, September 2019.

number of financial services provided to its citizens or organisations due to high risks and compliance costs, so blockchain can enhance financial inclusion in these countries, boosting the economic growth and living standards of its people. In addition, blockchain has great potential to enhance the adoption of clean and affordable energy resources in emerging markets and thus alleviate the negative impacts on climate and environment.

According to the World Bank Group, blockchain-based applications and services are springing up across Africa and Latin America and Asian countries like China are attracting an increasing number of blockchain investment. Companies and regulators in emerging economies need to work together to foster a nurturing innovation ecosystem and effectively manage the related risks and costs at the same time, paving the way for a potential technological leapfrog that burgeons financial inclusion and economic growth.[37]

4.4.2.3 *Energy and Climate*

Blockchain can improve a wide range of aspects in energy and environment protection initiatives. To name a few, it can improve the efficiency of existing grids by taking out the intermediary for energy exchange via the decentralised platforms and promote water and energy usage optimisations through usage tracking by users in a transparent and easily accessible platform.[38] Blockchain-based platforms can also be used to boost market innovation and efficiency for resources, such as carbon and other substances through crypto-tokens with tradable value, and generate new opportunities for carbon credit transactions.[39] Besides, companies can use blockchain for sustainability reporting, monitoring, and verification so that the clear accountability and reporting transparency can help enterprises make better-informed decisions about environmental-related issues.

[37] *"Blockchain: Opportunities for Private Enterprises in Emerging Markets"*, International Finance Corporation, World Bank Group, January 2019.

[38] *Ibid.*

[39] *"Building Block(chain)s for a Better Planet"*, World Economic Forum, September 2018.

An increasing number of companies working on providing blockchain solutions for environmental issues have emerged. For example, Power Ledger and Grid+ are revolutionising the energy industry by enabling peer-to-peer and intermediary-free energy trading for communities. Another company, SmartMesh, is exploring efficiency of food supply chain through blockchain to optimise food management and mitigate carbon emissions caused by food waste.[40]

4.5 Impact and Implications of Technology Trends in Singapore

Through the Smart Nation initiative, Singapore's investments in research, innovation, and enterprise lay the foundation for its Future Economy. Under Singapore's Research, Innovation, and Enterprise 2020 plan, an annual investment of around S$4 billion (US$2.8 billion) is used to facilitate research and innovation for a five-year period, to "win the future through science and technology".[41]

4.5.1 *Technology Investments in Singapore*

Singapore has been investing in emerging technologies in order to prepare for the future.

4.5.1.1 *Artificial Intelligence*

Singapore launched its National AI Strategy[42] in November 2019, which spells out the country's plans to deepen its use of AI technologies to transform its economy, going beyond just adopting technology, to also fundamentally rethink business models and make deep changes to reap productivity gains and create new areas of growth.

[40] "*6 Blockchain Startups Disrupting The Energy Industry*", StartUs Insights, December 2018.

[41] "*Research Innovation Enterprise 2020 Plan*", NRF, May 2019.

[42] "*National Artificial Intelligence Strategy*", Smart Nation and Digital Government Office, November 2019.

4.5.1.2 *Blockchain*

Singapore launched the Blockchain Ecosystem 2019 report[43] in November 2019. This report gives an overview presentation of Singapore's vibrant and diverse Blockchain landscape and showcases the substantial progress made by local public and private participants in Singapore.

4.5.1.3 *5G Communications*

Singapore is also investing in 5G communications to reinforce Singapore's position as a global business and connectivity hub. It is expected to roll out 5G mobile networks by 2020, with full-fledged 5G standalone capability covering at least half of Singapore by end 2022.[44]

In a joint-collaboration between IMDA and PSA Corporation Ltd, a live testing ground will be set up to gain a deeper understanding around the potential of 5G technology and integration capabilities in a Smart Port environment.[45] In addition, IMDA and Microsoft are also collaborating to set up a 5G development environment for government and industry players to co-create 5G use cases that can lead to the development of new 5G applications, services, and capabilities.[46]

4.5.1.4 *High-Performance Computing*

Singapore is also investing in the country's supercomputing infrastructure, with an investment of S$200 million announced in March 2019 to upgrade the infrastructure to provide research institutions and universities with wider access to high-performance computing (HPC) capabilities. This upgrade will provide 15–20 petaFlops of high-end computing performance

---

[43] *"Singapore Blockchain Ecosystem"*, IMDA, November 2019.

[44] *"Singapore Continues to Invest in Infrastructure, Partnership and Innovation to Boost our Digital Economy"*, IMDA, October 2019.

[45] *"M1 Joins IMDA and PSA to Test 5G Technologies in a Live Smart Port Environment"*, M1, June 2019.

[46] *"IMDA and Microsoft Collaborate to Accelerate the Development of Singapore's 5G Innovation Ecosystem"*, IMDA, November 2019.

STRENGTHS

1. Pro-business environment
2. Internationally trusted legal system and IP framework
3. Political stability
4. Technologically savvy consumers
5. Pro-open source environment, which has contributed to driving innovation in Singapore, e.g. in blockchain

WEAKNESSES

1. Small domestic market
2. Small population size constrains the volume of data available for AI model development

OPPORTUNITIES

1. AI research – Singapore universities amongst the top in ranking in citation impact[1]
2. Shift of AI from discovery phase to implementation phase[2] – Opportunities for Singapore to reap economic benefits of AI through driving adoption
3. Recognised as one of the top blockchain hubs[3] globally, creating opportunities for thought leadership
4. Neighbouring countries in ASEAN with large populations present tech providers in Singapore with ripe opportunities for technology adoption

THREATS

1. Need for Singapore to constantly keep abreast, due to dynamic and fast-moving pace of technological advancements globally and in neighbouring countries
2. Relatively more urgent need, compared to neighbouring countries in ASEAN, to address job displacement from technologies including AI and robotics[4]

NOTE: 1) "NTU Ranks Top 3 Globally in Citation Impact of AI Research", NTU, May 2017; 2) "What China can Teach the US about Artificial Intelligence", New York Times, Sep 2018; "5 Reasons why Singapore is a Famous Hub for Blockchain and Crypto Conferences", CoinStaker, Sep 2018; 4) A 2018 study conducted by Cisco and Oxford Economics indicated that within Southeast Asia, Singapore will be worst-hit by job displacement arising from technologies – Nearly 21% of full-time workers could be impacted

Figure 4.3. SWOT Analysis of AI, Data and Blockchain in Singapore.

for industry and academia to solve complex problems, including climate change prediction and urban planning.

4.5.2 *Opportunities and Challenges for Singapore*

Singapore has distinctive features that may boost or hinder technology adoption and advancements. These strengths and weaknesses in the areas of AI, data and blockchain are summarised in Figure 4.3.[47]

[47] "*Services and Digital Economy (SDE) Technology Roadmap*", IMDA, November 2018.

Annex A

Model AI Governance Framework

1 Introduction

The Model AI Governance Framework is an accountability-based framework to frame discussions around harnessing AI in a responsible way. It translates ethical principles into practical measures that can be implemented by organisations deploying AI solutions at scale. The Model Framework aims to promote AI adoption while building consumer confidence and trust in the AI technologies.

The following section provides an overview of the Model AI Governance Framework and more information is available at Personal Data Protection Commission (PDPC) Singapore.[1]

[1]The Model AI Governance Framework Second Edition can be downloaded from Go.gov.sg/ai-gov-mf-2.

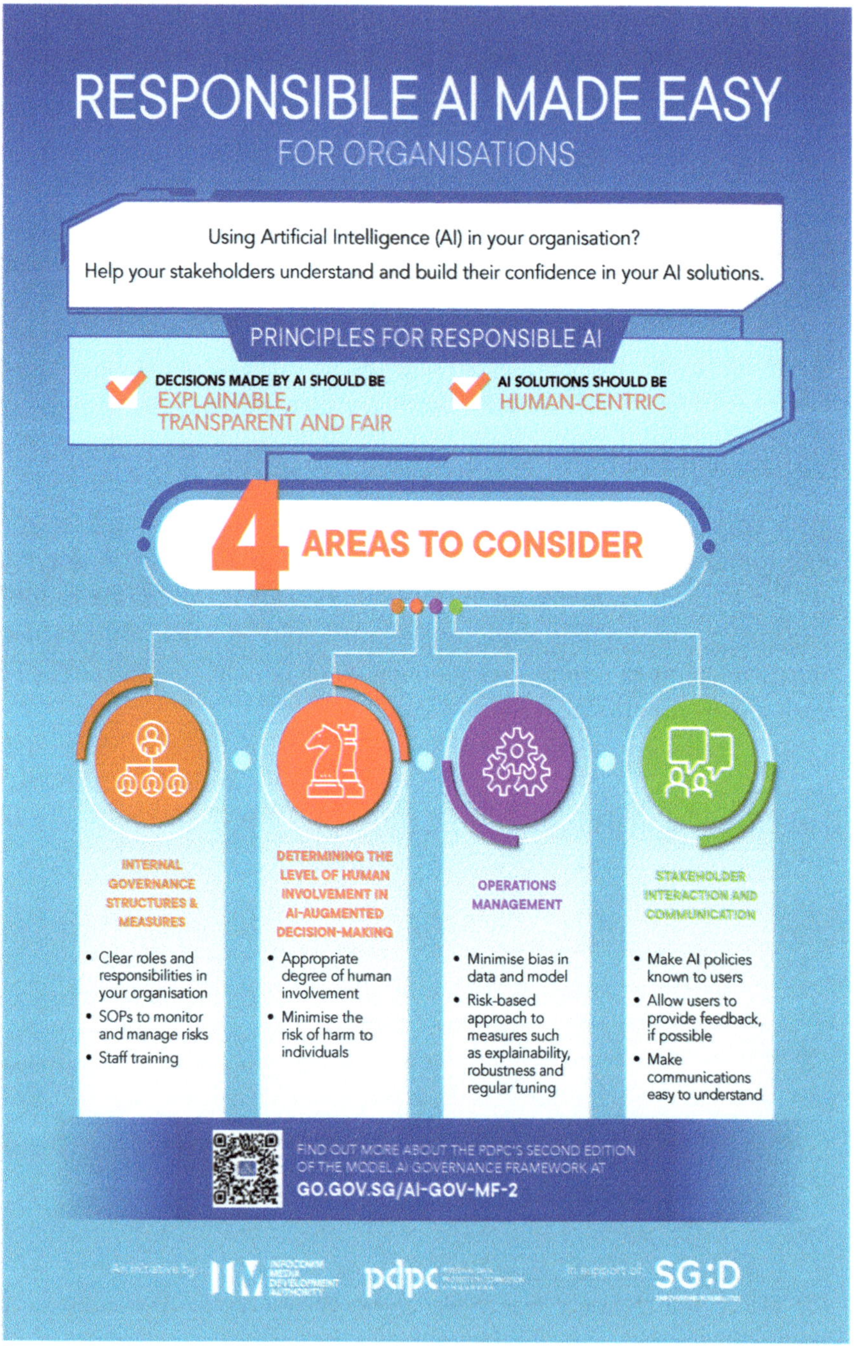
RESPONSIBLE AI MADE EASY
FOR ORGANISATIONS
Using Artificial Intelligence (AI) in your organisation?
Help your stakeholders understand and build their confidence in your AI solutions.
PRINCIPLES FOR RESPONSIBLE AI
DECISIONS MADE BY AI SHOULD BE EXPLAINABLE, TRANSPARENT AND FAIR
AI SOLUTIONS SHOULD BE HUMAN-CENTRIC
4 AREAS TO CONSIDER
INTERNAL GOVERNANCE STRUCTURES & MEASURES
• Clear roles and responsibilities in your organisation
• SOPs to monitor and manage risks
• Staff training
DETERMINING THE LEVEL OF HUMAN INVOLVEMENT IN AI-AUGMENTED DECISION-MAKING
• Appropriate degree of human involvement
• Minimise the risk of harm to individuals
OPERATIONS MANAGEMENT
• Minimise bias in data and model
• Risk-based approach to measures such as explainability, robustness and regular tuning
STAKEHOLDER INTERACTION AND COMMUNICATION
• Make AI policies known to users
• Allow users to provide feedback, if possible
• Make communications easy to understand
FIND OUT MORE ABOUT THE PDPC'S SECOND EDITION OF THE MODEL AI GOVERNANCE FRAMEWORK AT
GO.GOV.SG/AI-GOV-MF-2
pdpc
SG:D

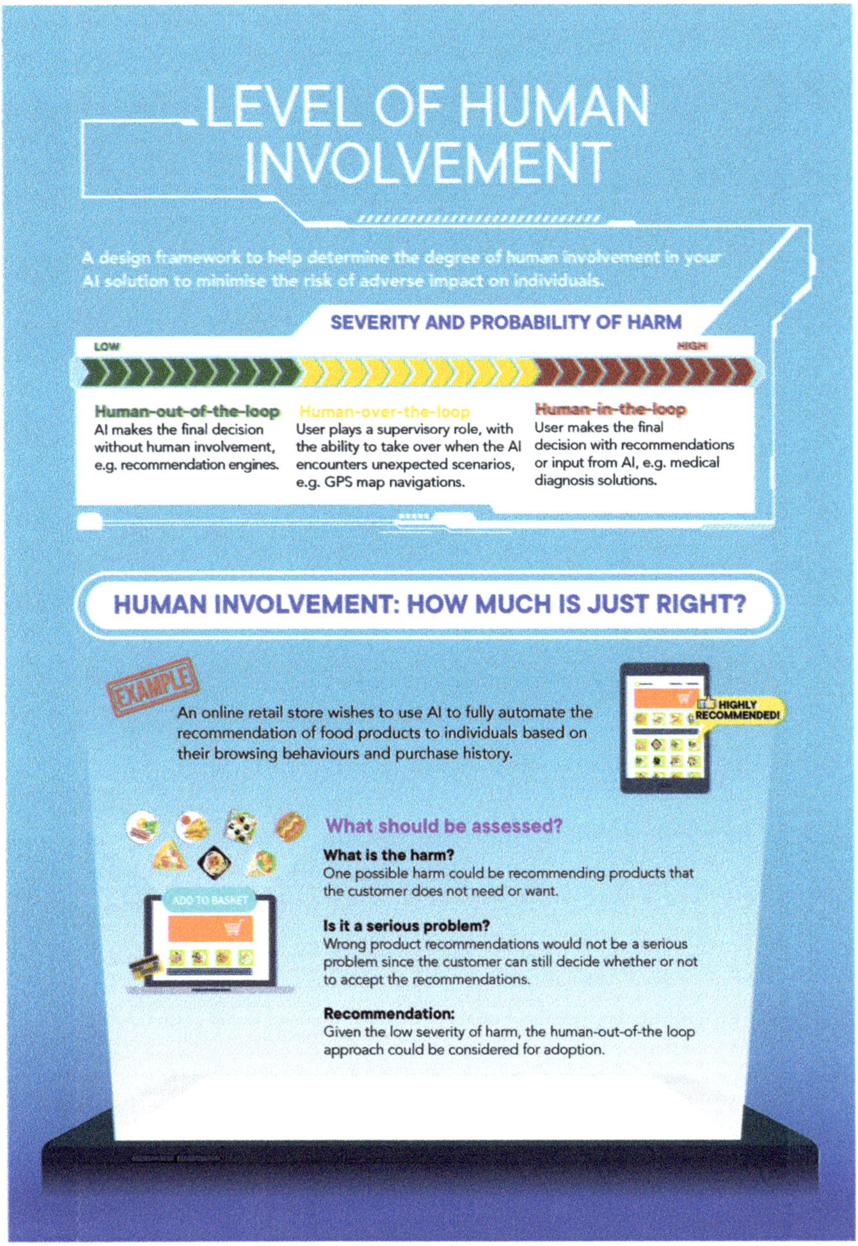
LEVEL OF HUMAN INVOLVEMENT
A design framework to help determine the degree of human involvement in your AI solution to minimise the risk of adverse impact on individuals.
SEVERITY AND PROBABILITY OF HARM
LOW
HIGH
Human-out-of-the-loop
AI makes the final decision without human involvement, e.g. recommendation engines.
Human-over-the-loop
User plays a supervisory role, with the ability to take over when the AI encounters unexpected scenarios, e.g. GPS map navigations.
Human-in-the-loop
User makes the final decision with recommendations or input from AI, e.g. medical diagnosis solutions.
HUMAN INVOLVEMENT: HOW MUCH IS JUST RIGHT?
EXAMPLE
An online retail store wishes to use AI to fully automate the recommendation of food products to individuals based on their browsing behaviours and purchase history.
HIGHLY RECOMMENDED!
ADD TO BASKET
What should be assessed?
What is the harm?
One possible harm could be recommending products that the customer does not need or want.
Is it a serious problem?
Wrong product recommendations would not be a serious problem since the customer can still decide whether or not to accept the recommendations.
Recommendation:
Given the low severity of harm, the human-out-of-the loop approach could be considered for adoption.

Annex 1

Transcript of Speech by Prime Minister Lee Hsien Loong at Smart Nation Launch, 24 November 2014

Minister Yaacob Ibrahim, Minister for Communications and Information
Minister Vivian Balakrishnan, Minister for Environment and Water Resources
Ms Yong Ying-I, Chairman of Infocomm Development Agency

Ladies and Gentlemen

May I congratulate all the winners of the National Infocomm Awards. You exemplify the spirit of innovation. You have brought technology and bright ideas together. You have made it work and you have made life better for us.

At this year's National Day Rally, I spoke on how we can use technology to make a difference to our people's lives, and to build a Smart Nation. Today, I am glad to be here to recognise the organisations and the people at the forefront of this effort. I will take a few minutes today to talk about our Smart Nation initiative and our vision for where we want to take Singapore in this direction.

Why Smart Nation: Our Vision

In 50 years since independence, we have succeeded beyond expectations. Soon after Separation Mr Lee Kuan Yew said — "Over a hundred years ago, this was a mud-flat swamp. Today this is a modern city. Ten years from now, this will be a metropolis. Never fear." Indeed Singapore has become a metropolis, and more. We have improved our standard of living. We have created opportunities for our people and we have built a city and country to be proud of.

Looking ahead, we should aim to be an outstanding city in the world. An outstanding place for people to live, work and play in, where the human spirit flourishes. The world is changing fast. We are a leading city today but other leading cities like San Francisco, New York, London, Sydney, Shanghai, they are attracting capital, talent, ideas. They are building outstanding urban environments. They are pulling ahead of the rest of the pack and even of the rest of the countries which they belong to. We have to move ahead with them and stay up there amongst the leading cities of the world. We owe it to our people and we can do this. We have the people, we have the resources and we have the ability to make it happen.

One important advantage which we have which we must take full advantage of is to use technology extensively and systematically, particularly IT. Not just piecemeal, individual gadgets, individual programmes and systems — that we are already doing, and all sorts of devices and applications have technology and IT in them. I am sure just in this room if we add all our handphones together we will have terabytes of storage and gigabytes of processing power but we have to do this systematically, to make the most of the potential, to integrate all of the technology and possibilities into a coherent and comprehensive whole. This will make our economy more productive, our lives better, and our society more responsive to our people's needs and aspirations.

Therefore our vision is for Singapore to be a Smart Nation — A nation where people live meaningful and fulfilled lives, enabled seamlessly by technology, offering exciting opportunities for all. We should see it in our daily living where networks of sensors and smart devices enable us to live sustainably and comfortably. We should see it in our communities where technology will enable more people to connect to one another more easily and intensely. We should see it in our future where we can create possibilities for ourselves beyond what we imagined possible.

We have already started on this Smart Nation journey. We are wired up and well-connected — 9 out of 10 Singapore homes have broadband and soon we should have fibre to every home. Our smart phone penetration is one of the highest in the world — 85 percent of people have smartphones. We are doing a lot in terms of e-government — IRAS' e-filing, MHA's Passport Application Services, NLB book borrowing — they are amongst the best in the world in terms of responsiveness, in terms of comprehensiveness of service. Nobody enjoys paying taxes but if you must pay taxes, pay to IRAS. In healthcare our public hospitals have integrated their patient records so that doctors can pull up information on the patient regardless of the hospital the patient goes to. If he is admitted as an emergency or he goes to another hospital, the data is there. Some other countries have spent tens of billions of dollars trying to build systems like this and sometimes giving up after spending tens of billions of dollars. We are not completely there yet but we are making progress and we are getting it to work. Our start-up scene is lively; there are more young people are starting companies, writing apps and building high-tech products and our people are technology-savvy. If you look at our schools math and science standards by all the international comparisons are amongst the best in the world. One positive sign is that not only have they got the aptitude, they are showing more interest in it. In the last three years, more of our best students have chosen to do Computer Science and Information Systems in our universities.

So we have the elements but we have to build on them to make a national effort, and to set ourselves the goal of becoming a Smart Nation. What does this mean? There are many things but let me just illustrate some the possibilities.

Our Daily Living

First of all, our daily lives should become more convenient and sustainable. Megan just now on video showed you what this means but let me tell you again. If you can automate the things which are routine we can focus our time and energy on the things that really matter to us.

We are developing Jurong Lake District into a beautiful location. Imagine how technology can contribute to this. Take a family heading down to Jurong Lake for a day out on a weekend. You are rushing and in your rush, you forgot to turn off your lights and your air-conditioner. In the old days, you either run all the way home or wait till the end of the day and kilowatt hours are burnt and money spent. But today you should be able to get your iPhone, connect to your home and find out what the status is and if your air-conditioning is on, turn it off, and if your lights are on, turn them off. Save energy, save bills, save anxiety. You may be unsure how you want to get to your destination so you get hold of an app and that tells you which bus and train to take and how to minimise the crowds. If you have a bigger family, lots of kids, you want to take a car; you should be able to get a self-drive car to take you there. No need to drive, no need to find parking! Along the way you should have a smooth ride because hopefully driverless cargo vehicles and container trucks move at night, driverless when the roads are free. Day time is freed up for people. And when you get there and you want to buy something, you just wave your watch to pay, and your watch will find the best credit card promotion! So instead of a PAssion card we should have a PAssion watch.

What I described is not really that far-off. In fact many technologies are already here. We already have smart devices in homes — whether air conditioners or lighting, they are there. We already have data and apps to help commuters plan their routes on buses and trains. In fact, LTA has just launched a new application to help you get from point A to point B and know how to do it. And I have one here, let me show you — I hope it works.

We have got the app on the screen, it is MyTransport at the bottom right, just click on it. This is the new version, you may already have one but this one showed up in the app store just last night. So if you have not updated your phone, please do so. The point is, this one has got a journey planner — the icon is at the bottom left, if you click on the journey planner, it shows you where you are, what your nearest bus stop is and you can choose where you want to go to. So we are at Marina Bay Sands at Bayfront Avenue and I want to go to Ion Orchard. It tells me that I must take bus 106 heading towards Bukit Batok Interchange. To get to bus 106, I need to walk to Marina Bay Sands Theatre which is across the road, take the bus, and when I get off the bus, I will walk to the destination at Orchard Turn and it will tell you how long you take to get there. As you sit on the bus, it will tell you how many stops to go, so from where you are, we have nine more stops to go and as you proceed, it will count down. You do not need to look at it all the time because two stops before where you are supposed to get off, it will beep and you can wake up — I hope so. I think LTA passes the test on this one, so do I.

You have got the apps, you have got driverless cars — they are coming. People see them as Sci-Fi but in fact they exist. Google has got their driverless car so have other companies. The Google one has driven 1 million kilometres and I hear they only had two accidents in that 1 million kilometres. One, they got rear-ended by a human being and the other one, a human being was driving the car and crashed it. So it will be some time before we all have driverless cars, but the technology is coming and we should all be ready for it.

We are trying out driverless buggies at the Lake District in Jurong and we will be trying out other driverless vehicles on some routes in One North next year. For transactions, the watch is not there yet but many of us already interact with Government departments online, like Tax-filing. We have been trialling NFC payments for retail and transport. We do not have to wait for ApplePay which was just launched in the US. What we need to do is to pull all these pieces together. For example, HDB is studying how to plug-and-play smart devices for the household, and to improve things that bother people, like parking allocation in HDB carparks. IDA is already building the network that will connect intelligent devices across the nation, from sensors to driverless cars. So that is how you can integrate everything seamlessly in our design of towns and our daily living.

Our Communities and Society

But being a Smart Nation is more than just making our lives more convenient, it can also strengthen our community and society, help us to connect to those we care deeply about. Enable us to do things we never imagined we could do, and empower communities to look out for and help one another.

Many of us are already on social media, the very old ones not so much, the not so old ones, probably on Facebook accounts. The very young ones think that Facebook is for old folks, so they do not do Facebook because their parents do it — so they are on Instagram and Twitter. Good and bad things come on social media but one good thing is that they help us to keep in touch with our friends and people whom we may not meet very often. But some lament that we spend too much time on Facebook and Twitter and Instagram and we need more face-to-face, and we have an app for that also. Made by Republic Polytechnic students, it is called Apple Tree. If you spend time with family and not touch your phones, you get a reward. So what we need to do is to integrate the online part with the real life offline part in order to create more opportunities for us to interact with one another. For example, we can have platforms where communities can come together to work on improving their precinct or provide feedback to government agencies on issues, on problems which need to be solved.

We can connect to our neighbours with apps, so that we can informally help one another. Like-minded neighbours can come together to pursue some common hobby like gardening or exercise together. Or you can share things or cooperate with one another like blockpooling.sg where you kind of have an exchange and you can do favours for one another or run errands for each other.

So these are all things which previously were quite impossible, but now they are possible. And one aspect of life which IT can make a big difference to is looking after the old people. Many of us have elderly parents to take care of, and we worry about their health and worry for their safety — if something happens to them, if they fall down or they get ill, we may not know. Because many seniors want to live alone, or rather, want to live in their own homes, instead of being completely reliant on others or their children.

If it may be two old folks and one passes on and it is one old person, in fact, 10–15 percent of our households are single person households. It is quite a thought, they have families but their families are not living in the same household as them. So we need to do something to solve this problem. HDB is piloting the Smart Elderly Monitoring and Alert System, I do not know what the acronym is but it is the Smart Elderly Monitoring and Alert System sensors in HDB flats, which uses a combination of sensors so that if the system detects something out of the ordinary, the routine changes, there was a signal where it should not have been, it can raise the alarm and alert family members or neighbours.

We can also use IT for tele-medicine, so that it can deliver healthcare to the home. The daughter does not have to travel all the way, or the nurse of the physio-therapist, but from the hospital we can connect up and you can talk and find out what is happening, and give advice and monitor and treat the patient.

I wanted to do a demonstration but instead of doing a demonstration, I will show you a video of how this is done, where the physiotherapist in the hospital can monitor and treat a stroke patient at home, watch the video, it tells you a heart-warming story. Video plays.

This is just one patient and she is not that old, but there are a lot of old people in Singapore who are at risk of this. By 2030, there is going to be 900,000 people in Singapore, 65 and over, and I think including many who are in this room. Our Smart Nation vision can radically change how we approach the idea of active ageing, so that we have more to look forward to in our golden years. We will also use technology in an inclusive way, so that all groups can benefit, including those not so familiar with IT, and in particular the older people.

We are going to have Citizen Connect Centres with officers to help citizens access Government services, while we make these services available online. We will have "Silver Infocomm Junctions" that provides affordable and customised IT training for seniors. When we have IT, we want it to be accessible to everybody and we have to prevent a digital divide from turning up in Singapore — between those who have IT and can afford it and know how to use it, and those who do not have IT or do not know how to use it. For example, we have e-filing for our courts — documents are filed electronically and stored in a database, you do not have to have stacks and stacks of paper. We move faster than other countries on this. I just met in Australia, the Governor of the State of Queensland, I was there for a meeting in Brisbane, and he used to be the Chief Justice of Queensland. He came to Singapore two years ago for a conference of Chief Justices and saw our system. He was very impressed. He said the most impressive thing was not that you have a computer system, but we have provided ways and booths where people who cannot afford the access and do not know how to do the access, they can go there and bring their papers there and they can be helped and have their papers filed electronically. You may be rich, you may be poor, if you have to go to the courts, if you need to have access to justice, you get access to justice. This was one issue that they in Queensland have thought about automating and computerising their filing, and how to make sure everybody has it. We have that and we must continue to have that.

Our Future

The Smart Nation is not just a slogan — It is a rallying concept for all of us to work together to transform our future together. I have just described a few ideas, these are just scratching the surface because there are endless possibilities waiting to be dreamed of.

We will only make this a Smart Nation if we get everybody active, engaged, excited, wanting to make this happen. When enterprises seize opportunities to provide a service or build a product that makes our lives better, when programmers build apps that help communities to bond, when neighbours step up to check on their neighbours through the HDB Smart Elderly monitoring system when it sounds the alarm.

The Government will lay the foundation — we will build the infrastructure, facilitate innovation and create the framework for all of us to contribute. One way in which we are going to do this, is to open up our maps, our databases of places and information about them, so that the public can share their geo-spatial information, can share meaning can use what is there and can contribute and put information into the system.

Imagine if we can tap on everyone's local knowledge and anyone can contribute data: animal sightings, traffic incidents, potential hazards for cyclists, even the best mee pok or nasi lemak.

Today, we are going to launch a new project called Virtual Singapore, the idea is to develop an integrated 3D map of Singapore enriched with layers of data about buildings, land and the environment. It will be a platform to bring the Government, Citizens, Industry and Research Institutions together to solve problems, for example to simulate wireless coverage or effects of heavy rain. What that means is to find out where it floods when it rains.

What We Will Do

To realise this vision, I think we have to pull the pieces together from all over the Government. We will set up a Smart Nation Programme Office. Today, the Government departments are all variously doing their own thing — LTA, URA, MOM and so on. Our research institutes are doing their own things, R&D institutes like A*Star are doing things like helping NLB sort books at night using robotics and sensors, quite interesting programmes, but we need to bring them together. We can go much further if we can put it together, to identify issues, prototype ideas, deploy them effectively to benefit the whole nation.

We will have a Smart Nation Programme Office and it will do this — take in perspectives and ideas from many sources, make sure that we take a whole-of-Government, whole-of-nation approach to building a Smart Nation. To make sure that it works, I am going to put this Office in the Prime Minister's Office, and I am putting Minister Vivian Balakrishnan in charge and I will take a personal interest.

One important aspect of a Smart Nation is cyber-security. We are outing more and more functions and data into our computers, handphones, networks and systems. Often they know more about us than we remember about ourselves. It is vital that we have secure systems that we can trust, not just preventing credit card numbers from being stolen, but protecting ourselves from malicious attacks where there is hacking or Distributed Denial of Service attacks, you know what that is. Whether is it malware that infects our computers which steals sensitive information or possibly threatens critical infrastructure if it gets into the hospital IT systems, patients can die, if it gets into our power system, our power grid can be brought down, if it gets into our airport system, we can have a very serious problem. In fact in America, there was one airport where a young teenager got into the airport IT system and rummage around, and was able to turn off all the airport lighting on the tarmac for half a day. So it is not a laughing matter, we take it seriously; we already have cyber security duties residing in Ministry of Home Affairs and the Infocomm Development Authority. But I do not think that they are as strong as we would like them to be. We need to reorganise them, to strengthen our system and our institutions. We are studying how best to do that, to protect our Government systems, including the Smart Nation sensor systems, against cyber-attacks. But also outside the Government, other critical systems like in telecoms, banking and energy sectors. You will never be completely impregnable, but I think we need to be secure and as safe as we can be. That means within the Government we need the system and outside the Government we must reach out to the companies and individuals, to raise your security awareness in order to create a secure and trusted ICT network.

We need the right organisations, the right skills, the right mindsets to be a Smart Nation. We have to start with our education system. We are equipping students with up-to-date knowledge and skills to use the technology. But schools must also teach students how to create the technology of the future; teach them to code, to prototype and build things, to fail fast and learn quickly, to use the latest gadgets, the latest tools and be up with the latest technology.

There is work being done on this all over the world. I just read an article — there is an American group which is designing a $10 robot, $10 for school children to learn how to programme robots. It can find out where it is, it can follow lines, it can move forward, move back, can turn, can measure distances using infrared, and you can programme it graphically. So if you want to turn the light on, you pull a LED icon, put it there, put the green light, it lights up. Children can do that. Our children can do that. We have kids in school who do very well at robot soccer. We never win, or we have so far not won at the real World Cup, but at the robotics world cup championships, we do very well.

I think that we must get our children in schools exposed to IT, exposed to programming. It is a long way for us, but in some countries, all kids are required to learn to code, at least the basics, so you understand what it is about, even though you may not write the next Windows operating system. We may not go that far, but I think we must expose our kids and we must enable the most talented and interested ones to be able to go far and develop their talent in IT in schools and pursue that, whether in university, whether after that, to set up a start-up or to join a company, or work with the Government and make a Smart Nation.

So we need the skills, we need the education, and the "can-do" spirit of experimenting and risk-taking. This is what makes Silicon Valley special: the world leader in technology innovation, a constant churn of ideas, of new business models. The Chinese are getting there too. I was in Shenzhen a few months ago, and visited Tencent, 腾讯, in Shenzhen. They are one of the big IT companies in the world now. If you walk around and talk to their people and soak up the mood, you would think you were in Silicon Valley. It is informal, it is casual, lots of energy, lots of new things going on — some will succeed, some will fail, but a passion to change the world. They put up screens showing all the places where people are using QQ or Wechat, and it is all over the world. I think we need that passion and that excitement to move.

Within the Government, we are reviewing how to manage the careers of our technologists and engineers, because we need to strengthen our own capabilities within the Government. We cannot just be outsourcing everything. Yes, we need to bring in expertise from the industry, but we need our own expertise too, not least to be able to specify what we want and to be able to interact fruitfully with the industry. In particular we will build up the IDA, because it has a key role in spearheading the development of a Smart Nation. Build up, meaning not just the headcount, but growing a culture and the mindset of experimentation. Being willing to try new approaches, disrupt existing ways of doing things; try, fail fast, learn the lessons, turn around quickly; constantly pushing the boundaries, inside the Government, outside the Government.

IDA needs more of this ethos. It cannot quite be like a Silicon Valley company, because it is not just a start-up. It has a regulatory role in telecoms; it has responsibilities in maintaining large Government systems. But IDA must also push the envelope, using technology to seek new applications, to find new approaches to existing problems. You must have that ethos within the system, within IDA. You must have that kind of people within IDA who want to do it and who feel that they can work like that, even though IDA is quite a big organisation and the Singapore Government has on-going responsibilities to keep the system going reliably and not failing.

Smart Nation is a lot of possibilities, I think, a lot of excitement, particularly for young people. This is our country, this is our future. My question to young people would be: Do you want to be part of this movement, to build a Smart Nation? Come together, design the solutions, test the ideas, give us the feedback, imagine it, let's decide on it, let's make it happen.

Conclusion

We are making a home for all Singaporeans, young and old. Not just the technologically savvy, but everyone. We want to transform our lives for the better, and we have what it takes to achieve this vision — the capabilities and the daring to pull it all together and make a quantum leap forward. I am looking forward to living in a Smart Nation — better living for all of us; stronger communities in our society; and more opportunities for all.

If I may go back to what Mr Lee Kuan Yew said when first we became independent and take it one step forward, update it, today perhaps this is what he would say: 50 years ago, we built a modern city. Today, we have a metropolis. 10 years from now, let's have a smart nation!

Let us make it happen together! Thank you very much.

Annex 2

Speech by Mr S Iswaran, Minister for Communications and Information at the Singapore Digital (SG:D) Industry Day, 21 May 2018

Mr Andre Hoddevik, Secretary General of OpenPEPPOL,

Industry Partners,

Fellow Colleagues,

Ladies and Gentlemen,

Imperative for digitalisation

1. Good morning. Let me start by warmly welcoming all of you to IMDA's inaugural Singapore Digital (SG:D) Industry Day.
2. The aim of this event is to demonstrate to industry players, like you, how you can participate in Singapore's journey of digital transformation. To show that businesses — of any size, in any sector, and at any stage of digitalisation — can seize opportunities and boost growth in the digital economy.
3. Aligned with our Smart Nation vision, the government is working with industry to chart Singapore's path towards digital transformation. The advent and adoption of disruptive technologies has revolutionised the global economy, changed business models and the nature of jobs. It has also created new possibilities for our businesses and for

Singapore's development. At the enterprise level, going digital can help companies increase productivity, achieve greater scale, serve customers better and generate new streams of earnings.

4. To maximise such benefits, digitalisation must be pervasive, cutting across all sectors so as to raise the capacity and competitiveness of the entire Singapore economy. That is why we are pursuing new and enhanced initiatives, to uplift all our businesses through digitalisation.
5. The Digital Economy Framework for Action charts our way forward and outlines our efforts to build Singapore's digital competitiveness and become a global node in Asia. IMDA will share more about the strategies and programmes laid out in the document.

Adoption of digital technologies across sectors

6. While the digital economy holds much promise, going digital may be daunting for many enterprises, especially given the challenges of today's complex and competitive economic landscape. Some companies find it difficult to even take the first step towards digitalisation. Others have already started and gained some momentum, but need help to go further in their digitalisation journey. We want to help all our companies succeed in this transformation, and are thus ramping up our efforts to accelerate the adoption of digital technologies.

SMEs Go Digital project management services

7. While the whole economy can gain from digitalisation, some segments may face greater challenges in making this transition. A case in point are our SMEs. Collectively, they employ two thirds of the workforce and contribute half of Singapore's GDP. Hence, digitalisation of SMEs can have a profound impact on our economy. Yet, our SMEs may be constrained by a lack of scale, resources or expertise.
8. It is precisely for this reason that the SMEs Go Digital programme was conceived — to make it simple for SMEs to digitalise. Today, SMEs Go Digital has helped close to 1,000 SMEs. This is an encouraging start but we can and must certainly do more to raise our SMEs' digital capabilities.

9. The challenge does not lie merely in the adoption of digital technologies. Rather, the greater challenge lies in sustaining the momentum and adapting to the fast changing environment. In other words, SMEs need to be able to effectively implement digital solutions to reap the full rewards of digitalisation. This means reviewing business processes, redesigning job roles and managing the transition to a digital paradigm. However, many SMEs do not have the requisite expertise to do this.
10. Therefore, we are enhancing the SMEs Go Digital efforts to make such expertise available to SMEs. IMDA is working with other government agencies, NTUC, and the Singapore Manufacturing Federation (SMF), the first pilot operator, to offer digital project management services for SMEs. We will train, certify and deploy experienced PMEs as in-house digital project managers. SMEs embarking on digital projects can also receive funding support for such services.
11. As a trial, the Singapore Manufacturing Federation (SMF) has provided digital project management services to businesses in Kampong Glam. IMDA's Kampong Glam digitalisation project is under way, and a key initiative is to drive merchants' adoption of integrated point-of-sale (POS) systems. The digital project managers have guided two F&B businesses, KokonoE ('ko-ko-nay') and Gloria Jean's Coffees, to implement POS systems, helping them modify their processes to maximise business outcomes. We look forward to many more companies emulating their success. To this end, IMDA will continue to explore other partnerships with industry to support the digital transformation of our SMEs.

E-invoicing and the adoption of PEPPOL standard

12. We also need shifts at the system level to be better prepared for the digital economy. E-invoicing is one example. Invoicing is a common and essential aspect of business transactions in the economy. E-invoicing can be adopted by all businesses as they begin their digitalisation journey, and serve as a shared reference point for the whole economy.

13. Traditional invoicing is manual, prone to human error, and can be costly for businesses. For instance, logistics firm GOGOVAN handles hundreds of corporate deliveries daily, with separate invoices for each client which can take up to eight days to process. GOGOVAN, and similar companies, can benefit from e-invoicing, which would help to cut costs, accelerate invoice processing and shorten payment times. Moreover, companies would also have real-time visibility of payment cycles, allowing them to better manage cash flows.
14. Despite these obvious benefits of e-invoicing, it has been challenging to drive its mass adoption to achieve network effects. This is because e-invoicing is currently fragmented, with many solutions that are proprietary and not interoperable. That is why we have been studying the development of an e-invoicing framework.
15. Today, I am happy to announce that we will be implementing the Pan-European Public Procurement On-Line (PEPPOL) as the nationwide e-invoicing standard in Singapore. Through this interoperable and low-cost standard, Singapore companies can more easily adopt e-invoicing on a large scale. In addition, this will help our companies transact internationally, with businesses from many other countries that are also in the PEPPOL network.
16. Our Government will lead the way for adoption, with agencies connecting government systems and processes, such as Vendors@Gov, to the framework. The National Trade Platform is exploring how to make PEPPOL one of the key international standards for trade documents accepted on the platform. Other government agencies supportive of the framework include the Accountant-General's Department, GovTech and the Maritime and Port Authority of Singapore.
17. From industry, many large players and associations have recognised the benefits of e-invoicing, and are looking to integrate their organisations, partners and members into the framework. For example, in the retail foods sector, lead buyers like NTUC FairPrice and Dairy Farm are keen to adopt the standard and help bring their suppliers on board. There are already over 40 companies who are keen to participate.

18. Together with the Singapore Business Federation (SBF) Digitalisation Committee and Enterprise Singapore, we will promote e-invoicing across the wider business community. Ultimately, the benefit of e-invoicing lies in scale of the network, and the breadth and depth of its adoption. Hence, it is important that all companies participate in and benefit from e-invoicing.

Building digital capabilities of the media sector

19. Beyond such system level initiatives, and our work with SMEs, we also need sector-specific responses to digital transformation. Whole sectors are being disrupted by technology, redefining business models and jobs. Our response must be to help our sectors move up the digitalisation ladder by building deep capabilities. Over the past few months, we have shared our plans to transform the ICM sector. Today, let me focus on how we aim to develop a competitive media sector through digitalisation.
20. New technologies, changing consumption patterns, and new entrants (such as Over-The-Top streaming platforms and integrated ecosystem players) are disrupting the media industry globally. Local media companies must acquire new capabilities to stay competitive in this evolving landscape.
21. To support the media sector in this endeavour, we are introducing an enhanced suite of programmes under our Future of Media strategy. One key programme is to deepen the content creation capabilities of our media companies. We will work with partners to help media companies harness technologies such as data analytics or AR/VR, to produce engaging content for an increasingly digital audience.
22. In addition, we will help our companies leverage the significant potential of digital streaming platforms. For instance, home-grown and Emmy-nominated series Oddbods, produced by One Animation, has been picked up for distribution by Netflix and Amazon Prime Video. Additionally, Oddbods' videos have accumulated 3.5 billion views on YouTube and other digital platforms. We want their success to inspire more companies to explore new streaming platforms to enhance outreach.

23. I would like to urge media companies to work closely with us, to nurture an innovative and competitive media sector that creates quality content and harnesses new technologies.

Development of innovative digital products and business models

24. We must also recognise that this age of disruption offers possibilities for experimentation with new digital products, services and business models. Fortune will favour those who embrace the change and are nimble and creative in their response.
25. Hence, we must set our sights higher. Beyond adopting technologies and building capabilities, we want to support our companies in taking the next big step in innovation and experimentation, to tackle complex business challenges and seize new growth opportunities.
26. One initiative to drive such efforts is the Open Innovation Platform (OIP), which was announced at Budget this year. The OIP will bring together tech companies and user companies to develop innovative solutions for real business problems. This will give local ICM companies opportunities to collaborate with diverse industry players, and create digital solutions that can be scaled and exported. IMDA will share more on the progress of the OIP.

Catalysing digital platform businesses

27. The digital revolution has also given rise to new technology-enabled, platform-driven business models, which have had a profound transformative impact on the digital economy. These digital platforms create value by aggregating ecosystems of end-users and producers, and using technology to facilitate transactions between them. Such platforms enable information sharing, collaboration and promote the creation of new products and services.
28. We have seen that digital platforms can enhance the delivery of AI and data services to different kinds of users. These range from companies that monetise data, to developers seeking data sets to build

applications, and end-user companies using apps to analyse data and derive insights. Hence, the growth of such platforms can generate value for many enterprises in the ecosystem.

29. But such platform businesses are not easy to build, and require time to cultivate its ecosystem of users before it can enjoy the benefits of network effects. Hence, to kickstart the development of platform networks in Singapore, IMDA will support companies to build innovative and commercially viable digital platforms that offer data and AI services to other players.
30. We have identified four companies to work with. One of these is DataStreamX, which operates a data transaction and marketplace platform. Through the digital platforms programme, DataStreamX will be enabling an AI and micro-services layer on top of its existing commercial platform. This will allow individuals or companies to build services on top of the data sources from the DataStreamX marketplace. Examples could include chatbots to solve business and consumer needs.
31. These are early days and these initiatives are just the beginning. Our businesses can expect more programmes that will help them generate value through innovation.

Conclusion

32. To conclude, I wish to emphasise that the goal of a productive, innovative and sustainable digital economy is well within our reach. The government looks forward to collaborating with industry to increase adoption, deepen capabilities and drive innovation. This will also put Singapore in good stead to enhance our economic competitiveness, and serve as an important global node for technology, innovation and enterprise.
33. As an economy and as a nation, we must continually reinvent ourselves to keep pace with the changes wrought by the digital economy, while capitalising on the multitude of
34. Thank you.

Annex 3

Speech by Minister S Iswaran, Minister for Communications and Information, at AI Singapore's 1st Year Anniversary Event, 30 August 2018

Good morning everyone.

1. I am pleased to join you today to celebrate the first anniversary of AI Singapore's formation. It has been an eventful year for AI Singapore and all its partners — companies, educational institutions, government agencies and our collaborators from abroad. I would like to thank all of you for helping AI Singapore get started on a strong footing.
2. AI Singapore was launched last year as a national programme to boost Singapore's artificial intelligence capabilities. It is a key initiative under the Services and Digital Economy (SDE) domain of our Research Innovation and Enterprise (RIE) 2020 plan, to enable Singapore and Singaporeans to benefit fully from the growth opportunities in the digital economy.
3. I would like to congratulate Professor Ho Teck Hua and his team at AI Singapore for their good work and accomplishments over the past year. You have heard from Prof. Ho about AI Singapore's progress in its three areas of focus — AI industry innovation, research and technology development.

4. AI Singapore has also helped to strengthen the linkages between industry and research, thereby ensuring that Singapore's research in AI remains pertinent to industry needs. 100Experiments is an example. It is a programme that not only fosters closer industry-research partnerships, but also innovates practical uses of AI to solve industry problems.
5. For instance, real-time and unpredictable events such as road accidents and sudden changes in driver or vehicle availability often pose problems to the transport industry. Versafleet is a local transport management software company that is exploring how AI could be used to better understand human behaviour and to develop optimised vehicle routing solutions. Such collaborations with industry are key to value creation by translating our investments in research and outcomes into practical solutions for problems faced by industry.

Key Message 1: Singapore will adopt a practical approach to build AI capabilities in a targeted fashion

6. With the increasing digitalisation of the global economy, AI will bring many more growth opportunities. This is why many countries, including the two largest economies the US and China, have significantly ramped up their investments in AI on multiple fronts. Singapore cannot and should not seek to emulate the scale and scope of their approach. Rather, we must identify and develop specific areas of focus that can yield the best returns on our investments, by building on our AI and other capabilities.
7. In this regard, one of Singapore's main strengths is our established and recognised R&D base in AI. Based on the Field Weighted Citation Impact of our research, AI Singapore is currently ranked first in the world. In May this year, the influential academic journal "IEEE Intelligent Systems" released its biennial "AI's 10 to Watch" list — 4 of these young stars are based in Singapore. Yet another strength is our growing and vibrant AI ecosystem. Through the efforts of the Economic Development Board (EDB) and Infocomm Media Development Authority (IMDA), we have seen an increase in the

number of both international and local companies with deep AI expertise that are thriving in Singapore. This includes industry giants like Alibaba as well as fast growing companies such as Taiger, Visenze and Data Robot. By leveraging these strengths in AI research and industry capabilities, Singapore is poised for the next moves in this exciting space.

Key Message 2: Singapore will double-down on AI talent development

8. Our first move will be to invest significantly in the development of AI **talent**. There is a consensus amongst governments, industry leaders and recruitment firms worldwide that there is a global shortage of AI talent. Singapore needs a deeper bench strength of talent to further grow our AI ecosystem. AI Singapore can and will play a key role in this regard by working closely with its research and industry partners to nurture a strong pipeline of AI talent in Singapore.
9. Last November, we launched the inaugural AI Apprenticeship Programme, a partnership between AI Singapore and the TechSkills Accelerator (or TeSA), which is a SkillsFuture initiative driven by IMDA and its strategic partners. The 1st batch of AI apprentices was inducted in May this year and they are in the midst of their training. All apprentices in this intensive programme, even those without a background in computer science, go through a combination of in-depth AI courses and on-the-job training on industry projects over the course of nine months.
10. One example is Eunice Soh, who is working with Surbana Jurong on a project to predict lift breakdowns using AI. Eunice majored in life sciences and does not have a computer science background. While the learning curve has been steep, the apprenticeship programme has helped Eunice and others like her to pursue their career aspirations in AI.
11. Building on the lessons from the first run, we will scale-up the AI Apprenticeship Programme so that more Singaporeans can obtain the

requisite training to become an AI engineer. The 2nd batch of apprentices will commence their programme in November this year.

12. While some firms require such AI engineers to develop, design and deploy AI solutions at-scale, we also need a differentiated approach to talent development to meet the industry's varied needs for AI capabilities. For instance, firms also need workers with a foundational understanding in AI and data science, which they can apply for business needs.
13. **[Announcement 1: AI for Industry Programme]** I am therefore pleased to announce that AI Singapore will launch AI for Industry, a three-month foundational programme for executives who are technically inclined and keen to learn programming to develop basic AI and data applications. Candidates will undergo a hybrid online and offline programming curriculum with a leading partner in this field, as well as face-to-face workshops.
14. To make it easier for individuals to pick up AI skills, AI Singapore will partner IMDA to reduce the cost of fees incurred by candidates. The AI for Industry Programme aims to train 2,000 AI users in three years' time.
15. **[Announcement 2: AI for Everyone Programme]** Beyond AI training, it is also important for everyone to develop a basic understanding of what AI and data science are about, and to be able to identify potential use cases at work and in our daily lives. To this end, AI Singapore will launch a free introductory programme, conducted in partnership with Microsoft, Intel and IMDA.
16. The AI for Everyone Programme aims to get 10,000 individuals exposed to AI and data science in three years' time. This introductory programme will help more individuals to appreciate the practical uses of AI and go a long way in ensuring that our companies and workers keep up with technological developments and emerging growth opportunities.
17. Through programmes like AI for Everyone, AI for Industry and the AI Apprenticeship Programme, we will develop a strong pipeline of AI talent for Singapore.

Key Message 3: Singapore will focus on building capabilities that can enable a trusted AI ecosystem

18. I have talked about our first move — talent. Our second move relates to **trust** — building a trusted AI ecosystem. As we all know, the growth of AI would require big data capabilities, and what has been categorised as privacy preservation technologies will be critical for the continued capitalisation of data. Increasingly, we need privacy solutions that can enable data integration across organisational boundaries. We also need more secure solutions, especially new methods of encrypting data on the public cloud.
19. This is one area which Singapore can target in our efforts to develop deeper AI capabilities. Singapore can build on our strong R&D base to develop a niche in privacy preservation technologies. We had earlier launched a grant call to build capability centres in this area of technological research, and the results will be announced shortly.
20. With the growing use of AI in our economy and workforce, it also important that we proactively address the ethical concerns that may arise, in order to develop a trusted AI ecosystem which can derive the benefits from the innovations that companies deploy whilst ensuring that we have the confidence of consumer acceptance. Hence, we announced the establishment of the Advisory Council on the Ethical Use of AI and Data led by Senior Counsel V.K. Rajah in June this year.
21. Today, I am happy to announce and welcome on board the rest of the council members. We have brought together international and local leaders, as well as advocates of consumer interests. They include:

    o **Ms Jenni Aldrich, Asia Pacific Vice President of Google;**
    o **Mr Amit Anand, Managing Partner of Jungle Ventures;**
    o **Professor Chan Heng Chee, Chairman of Lee Kuan Yew Centre for Innovative Cities at the Singapore University of Technology and Design;**
    o **Dr Chen Wei, Chief Operating Officer of Social Credits;**
    o **Mr Chia Song Hwee, President of Temasek International;**

- **Mr Andreas Ebert, Worldwide National Technology Officer of Microsoft Corporation;**
- **Mr Piyush Gupta, Chief Executive Officer of DBS Group;**
- **Ms Hamidah Aidillah Mustafa, Founder of Parrot Social**
- **Mr Peter Ho, Chairman of National Supercomputing Centre Steering Committee; and**
- **Ms Sara Yu Siying, Group Vice President, Deputy General Counsel and Partner of Alibaba.**

22. The Advisory Council will canvass widely for views, from businesses, trade associations and chambers, and consumers, and I look forward to the Advisory Council's recommendations on how organisations can develop and deploy AI solutions in a responsible and trusted manner.

Closing

23. In summary, I have spoken about our next moves on two fronts — talent and trust — to help build Singapore's AI capabilities and to position us well in the next stages of growth in this fast growing space. These efforts, to take advantage of opportunities brought forth by frontier technologies such as AI, are key to ensuring that our companies, researchers and workers continue to benefit from the increasingly digitalised economy.
24. Once again, my congratulations to AI Singapore and its partners on the good work and achievements in your inaugural year. We look forward to many more milestones and successes.
    Thank you.

Annex 4

Opening Remarks by Mr S Iswaran, Minister for Communications and Information at Tech Saturday (Upsized!), 2 June 2018, Singapore

SMS Dr Janil Puthucheary
Friends and colleagues from IMDA
The larger digital community of Singapore
Ladies and gentlemen
Good afternoon to all of you.

I am happy to join you here today at this year's Tech Saturday (Upsized!), where there is something for everyone here to experience in terms of technology, and how it is changing the way we live and work.

The Importance of Digital Readiness

2. We all know that technology has a major impact on our lives, and it is creating many opportunities for all of us, to connect with each other and to also enhance our lives. But we also know that there are segments of our community who — either because they are not familiar, or because they do not have access to the technology — may not be able to fully participate in technological change and enjoy the benefits that it can bring.

3. This year, President Halimah Yacob, at the re-opening of Parliament, highlighted that one of our Government's key priorities is to build a cohesive, caring and inclusive society. The true measure of a nation is not just how vibrant or strong our economy is but also how we care for one another in our society, in particular, how we provide the services that are necessary to those who are in need. Our housing, education and healthcare programmes have all been important pillars of this important national effort to ensure that every Singaporean is able to level up and share the fruits of our progress.
4. In the digital age, all nations face the challenge of a new divide — between the digital haves and digital have-nots. Digitalisation will have a profound impact on our quality of life — our access to opportunities, our ability to engage in social networking and in terms of the services that we can enjoy. So, we want to ensure that no one is left behind in this digital transition. We want to ensure that every Singaporean has the means, skills and the confidence to embrace digital technology to improve their lives.
5. That is why the Ministry of Communications and Information convened the Digital Readiness Workgroup last year — to examine how we can help Singaporeans to be more digitally ready. The Workgroup was led by SMS Dr Janil Puthucheary, and comprised senior representatives from the people, private and public sectors. I was informed that they had robust discussions, generated many ideas, and spoke to diverse stakeholders before coming up with their recommendations. Several members of the Workgroup are here today — please join me in recognising them for their hard work.

Launch of the Digital Readiness Blueprint

6. Today, I am delighted to launch the Workgroup's Digital Readiness Blueprint. This document contains strategies and recommendations that will enable Singaporeans to thrive in a Smart Nation. The Blueprint also contains specific recommendations to help the digitally vulnerable, the general public, as well as businesses and other organisations.
7. To help those who are less digitally-savvy, the Workgroup has recommended making basic digital access more widespread,

providing one-on-one assistance for digital queries, and identifying a set of Basic Digital Skills as a starting point. IMDA has recognised and accepted this, and has developed a curriculum for basic digital skills and will be offering this at selected Silver Infocomm Junctions. These skills include communicating, transacting and staying safe online. The first round of workshops based on the curriculum will be conducted at the Silver IT Fest from 22 to 24 June this year.

8. MCI and IMDA are also working with the Smart Nation and Digital Government Office, GovTech and the People's Association to have dedicated one-on-one assistance at community touch points, to reach out to Singaporeans who might need help to learn and use technology. We will be piloting this at some community centres in the latter half of the year. In the longer term, we hope to make this service available at many more community touchpoints. It needs to be ubiquitous like the Internet, if we have to make an impact in people's lives and lifestyles.
9. MCI is also studying the recommendation to provide widespread basic digital access carefully, with a view to defining the scope, identifying the people who might be more in need of a basic access package, and how best to meet their needs.
10. The blueprint is relevant not just for vulnerable groups, but also considers the needs of the wider community. The Workgroup has recommended stepping up efforts in information and media literacy, especially given the increasing problem of deliberate online falsehoods and scams. MCI is working on a national information and media literacy framework, pulling together the good work that is already being done in raising awareness and educating the public. These include the Media Literacy Council's Better Internet Campaign, the National Library Board's S.U.R.E. programme, the Cyber Security Agency's Go Safe Online, and others, to make sure that the curriculum is holistic and aligned.
11. Businesses and community organisations also have a big role to play in building digital readiness. One of the Workgroup's recommendations is to establish a Digital Participation Pledge, where organisations commit to building digitally inclusive services, and equipping their employees with digital skills. Those that are more advanced can

educate their customers and support wider digitalisation efforts in our society.

12. There were several recurring themes in the course of the Workgroup's engagements. One was the need for the human touch in the digital world. Another was the need to develop deep partnerships and collaborations between businesses, the community, and the government. And yet another was about ensuring that our digital readiness initiatives meet the needs and provide increased convenience for all Singaporeans. These are some of the guiding principles that we will bear in mind as we work across the public, private and people sectors to implement the Workgroup's recommendations.
13. Ultimately, the heart of every nation is our people. And we want to ensure that all Singaporeans can thrive and lead fulfilling lives in a digital era, using technology as a critical enabler.
14. All of us can play a part in this important endeavour. I want to invite everybody — those of you who are here, and many more important stakeholders — to participate actively and to also help your family, friends, and loved ones to become digitally ready — so that we can all come together to live, work and play in a Smart Nation.
15. I wish all of you an exciting and fun day at Tech Saturday.
16. Thank you very much.

Annex 5

DPM Teo Chee Hean at Opening of Smart Nations Symposium: Speech by DPM and Coordinating Minister for National Security, Teo Chee Hean, at the Smart Nation Innovations Week Opening Symposium on 5 June 2018

"Building a Smart Nation — Empowering Citizens, Energising Businesses, Engaging Internationally"

Your Excellencies,
Distinguished Guests,
Ladies and Gentleman,

I am happy to join you at the inaugural Smart Nation Innovations Week Opening Symposium. To our overseas guests, a warm welcome to Singapore.

Strong Foundation for Building a Smart Nation

Singapore has worked with like-minded regional and international partners over many decades to build an open and inclusive global environment for the exchange of ideas, the flow of trade and investments, and the deepening of people-to-people ties. Even as we continue to enhance physical connections in the traditional air, land and sea domains, the digital domain now offers new ways to interact, collaborate and form new partnerships; with exciting opportunities to grow our future economy and improve the lives of all our citizens.

Today, Singapore is one of the most networked economies in the world. We have invested in fibre broadband connectivity so that high-speed broadband mobile internet connectivity is available and affordable to companies and individuals all across Singapore. This physical infrastructure and connectivity provides the foundation. But new important back-end, whole-of-nation enabling systems, are needed to enable us to fully exploit these new technologies to create game-changing exciting new businesses and jobs, and to allow our citizens to enjoy access to public and private sector services in new ways that make a real difference to our daily lives.

What does Smart Nation mean to us, as citizens and businesses and for our international partnerships? Our Smart Nation journey has to improve daily life in our city and make it more convenient and secure; create exciting jobs and opportunities for everyone; and energise those who are able, creative and driven to pursue their dreams not only in Singapore, but with friends all around the world.

Empowering Citizens, Improving Lives

A Smart Nation has meaning when our citizens are more empowered, when we are able to take more control of and see real improvements in our day-to-day life experiences — better work-life balance, better use of our time, staying more aware and connected with our friends, smoother and faster commutes, taking charge of our healthcare and financial needs.

Smart Nation will be powered by technology — the enabling game-changer. But technology is not an end in itself. To achieve widespread use and benefits, the applications need to be seamless and intuitive to use, without the user needing to spend time to navigate the complex underlying technology. Let me illustrate with a few examples.

Many of us are already using wearables or our mobile apps to remind us to exercise, such as tracking whether we have walked our 10,000 steps today. We want to help more citizens stay fit and healthy. Citizens can manage their own diet and exercise, and decide what is more suited to their individual needs and contexts. For example, we can help our young working adults, including our National Servicemen maintain their fitness. Or we can monitor our vital signs or manage our medications with a personalised digital health coach; and be alerted to call in for a telemedicine consultation. This means that healthcare is not delivered only at the hospital or the doctor's clinic. We can re-design our healthcare system by working with our citizens to keep us all as fit and healthy as possible, while making best use of our healthcare resources. I would like to emphasise this last step because when we put together all these individual devices for the use by individuals, and re-design the entire healthcare system, that is where the real opportunity comes — systems-level efficiency and systems-level delivery, for high quality services to our citizens.

In our public housing estates where more than 80% of Singaporeans live, the use of the Internet of Things and analytics for preventive maintenance and municipal operations can help make the environment more liveable and sustainable. Sensors can help our households and estates save on utilities, and operators can do more targeted and timely maintenance to improve lift reliability or public cleanliness.

Today, we already use data and data analytics, together with a network of sensors and roadside cameras to keep residents safe and ensure that traffic is smooth. In future, with more data, for example from smart street lamps, and tools to better plan bus routes and improve car-pooling and bike-sharing, commuters can plan their journeys, save time and have a better, safer experience getting around our city for work or leisure. The Digital Readiness Blueprint launched by Minister for Communications and Information S Iswaran last weekend also outlined our plans to help all Singaporeans gain digital skills and use digital tools in their daily lives.

Our government services are also going through a major transformation to put our citizens at the centre. The objective is to make services intuitive and easy for all to use — in several languages, and even if we are less familiar with technology. At significant Moments of Life, for example, when welcoming a newborn to the family, parents will be able to select from a suite of public services from different agencies, including registering baby's birth and automatically enrolling baby onto relevant support schemes, such as the "baby bonus". Parents will also be able to find information about preschools, what they offer around their residence. We are releasing a blueprint for Digital Government today, outlining how the Government will reorganise and transform ourselves to deliver public services better through the use of technology. This involves improving the user-experience interface where citizens interact with a greater range of government e-services; but also important back-end, whole-of-nation enabling systems, such as SingPass Mobile, which will be rolled out as part of our National Digital Identity system which is being implemented later this year. This is a 2 factor authentication, PKI-based system which will enable our citizens to easily and securely transact with each other and access our government services without the need for physical tokens or SMS passwords. We can pay our bills or sign documents online, apply for public housing, buy or sell a house or a car.

Energising Businesses, Seizing Opportunities

A Smart Nation has meaning when our businesses can exploit new opportunities in the Digital Economy — this includes operating more efficiently, reaching out to new markets through digital platforms, and creating new businesses in sectors which were not available in the pre-Digital Economy.

There will be many exciting new jobs in the Digital Economy — in emerging technology like Artificial Intelligence or data science, but also from making use of commonly available digital tools or platforms to expand businesses in innovative new ways, or to create new businesses. There are now a whole range of programmes to help everyone be digitally ready and digitally skilled, from introductory programmes in the community to make best use of digital services, to those for the tech-experts at the sharp end of the new enabling technologies in our universities and research institutes.

To facilitate new opportunities and business models in the Digital Economy, the Monetary Authority of Singapore is working with industry partners to enhance our National e-Payments ecosystem. Our focus is on building common links at the back-end, while supporting a range of e-payment platforms at the user-interface. This will enable consumers and businesses to enjoy more convenience, flexibility and efficiency at the point of sale, whether physical or virtual. Simplicity of use at the front-end and integration at the back-end will help to make the overall e-payment ecosystem flexible, open and contestable — allowing new technology, and new payment platforms to come into the market to serve consumers and businesses better.

To help our businesses take full advantage of the Digital Economy, the Infocomm Media Development Authority is working with our businesses, industry associations and unions to accelerate digitalisation and build digital capabilities across our industries.

The Services and Digital Economy is also a focus area in our US$ 14 billion (S$ 19 billion) Research, Innovation and Enterprise 2020 Masterplan. We aim to spark digital innovation to support Advanced Manufacturing and Engineering, Health and Biomedical sciences, and Urban Solutions and Sustainability. For instance, we have strengths in Artificial Intelligence which are being applied in aircraft engine design and maintenance forecasting. Our medical researchers and data scientists are working together using the resources at our National Supercomputer Centre to develop precision medicine for our citizens in our future healthcare system.

Engaging Internationally, Forming Partnerships

The digital domain cuts across national boundaries. A Smart Nation also means that we collaborate with our international partners and other Smart Cities to deliver digital solutions that link and benefit people and businesses across boundaries.

Our national level-projects, such as the National Digital Identity and the e-payments infrastructure not only enable more secure and convenient digital services in Singapore, but also allow businesses to develop innovative new services and business models that can apply across borders and economies.

The National Digital Identity provides definitive proof of identity, not just physically face-to-face, but virtually over the Internet. Our e-payments infrastructure allows a trusted exchange of value to take place virtually — allowing parties who may otherwise be unknown to each other to transact reliably. This infrastructure enables the secure, trusted exchange of information and value that underpins digital commerce and digital transactions.

For instance, businesses can access trade finance instruments digitally to reduce time-to-market and save on transaction fees. We have recently adopted the Pan-European Public Procurement On-Line e-invoicing standard, to facilitate the exchange of machine-readable e-invoices. We are also working on a blockchain-based trade financing project with Hong Kong to enable trade-related digital transactions across borders. This will provide traders, banks and clearing facilities a common view to enable trusted transactions, and execute contracts faster.

At the same time, as economies become more integrated and connected digitally, we are also keenly aware of the rapid way in which cyber-threats evolve and grow. Our systems that underpin global commerce and finance are constantly being probed. The more interconnected we are, and the more we rely on such interconnected digital systems, the more vulnerable we are to not just a local disruption, but potentially a system-wide global one. For instance, the WannaCry ransomware attacks impacted more than 150 countries, affecting public healthcare systems and also key shipping lines, with knock-on effects on nodes which were themselves not attacked. The impact of WannaCry was not very dissimilar from the volcanic disruptions in Iceland several years ago, that not only disrupted air traffic in North- Western Europe, but also impacted air traffic globally. One of the international airlines that operates its call centre in Singapore was helping to re-route passengers who were affected. When the WannaCry ransomware affected some major shipping lines which had global operations, they operated out of Singapore as well as some of their digital tools were not available. Such knock-on effects on nodes and cyber attacks can be quite a global concern.

Our public agencies and companies in Singapore have been implementing cybersecurity defences that cover 11 Critical Information Infrastructure sectors — from aviation and energy, to healthcare and water supply. We conduct cybersecurity exercises every year to test the resilience of our systems as well as our collective operational responses. Last year, for the first time, we conducted a national exercise covering all the 11 Critical Information Infrastructure sectors. We will continue to explore joint exercises with our international partners, for example with global financial hubs to share experiences and raise our systemic capabilities to deal with cyber incidents and emergencies that have effects across borders. While these exercises are conducted on an annual basis, there is still much that can be done.

Under our ASEAN Chairmanship this year, I am glad that 26 ASEAN cities have come together to form a Smart Cities network to exchange experiences in using technology and digital solutions. This enables ASEAN cities to strengthen their inter-connectivity, and our industry partners to deploy and scale up solutions, to improve the lives of our people across ASEAN. I thank the ministers-in-charge of ICT in ASEAN and our dialogue partners, Digital Government and Smart City leaders for your strong support for the Network, and strengthening community-building in ASEAN.

Our Ministry of Communications and Information, together with our Smart Nation and Digital Government Office will continue to seek out international partnerships to share experiences, and explore collaborations.

Conclusion

A Smart Nation is about enabling our people and businesses to exploit the full potential of the new digital technologies to improve the lives of our people and provide more opportunities for our businesses.

This Smart Nation Innovations Week has brought together a strong community, including ICT Ministers, Government Chief Technology Officers, Smart City leaders, startups, investors and academics from Singapore and beyond to discuss how we can ride this digital wave together to benefit our citizens and businesses.

I trust that you will make full use of the opportunity to have productive exchanges over the coming days to strengthen connections, generate new ideas and create robust partnerships.

I wish you all a fruitful Smart and Innovative Week ahead. Thank you.

Annex 6

Remarks by Mr S Iswaran, Minister for Communications and Information, at the Joint Press Conference with World Economic Forum Centre for the Fourth Industrial Revolution on 21 January 2020

Good afternoon to members of the press and my fellow panel members. Delighted to be here at the joint press conference with WEF C4IR and industry partners.

2. Singapore, together with WEF and industry partners will be taking a big step forward today in AI governance. Collectively, we are building a trusted AI environment that will guide organisations to deploy AI responsibly.

Singapore's Approach to AI Governance

3. These efforts build on what Singapore had shared last year in Davos. Last year in Davos, Singapore launched the Model AI Governance Framework to guide businesses to deploy AI at scale in a responsible manner.

4. This framework translates ethical principles into pragmatic measures that businesses can adopt voluntarily, and have a ready-to-use tool to help deploy AI in a responsible manner.

5. A year on, the Framework has gained further traction and support.
   i. We have been working with WEF C4IR to promote the use of the Model Framework, including engaging companies locally and internationally on the World Economic Forum platforms.
   ii. International and local companies across diverse sectors have adopted or aligned their practices to it.

6. This year in Davos, I am pleased to announce today that Singapore is taking yet another step forward in AI Governance.

7. Together with our partners, we are releasing three AI governance initiatives to further guide organisations in deploying AI responsibly. These are the:
   i. Implementation and Self-Assessment Guide for Organisations (ISAGO)
   ii. Second edition of the Model Framework
   iii. Compendium of Use Cases

8. Let me elaborate.

Implementation and Self-Assessment Guide for Organisations (ISAGO)

9. As part of Singapore's collaboration with WEF C4IR to drive AI and data innovation, we have co-developed an Implementation and Self-Assessment Guide for Organisations (ISAGO).

10. This guide will help organisations assess the alignment of their AI governance practices with the Model Framework. It also provides an extensive list of useful industry examples and practices to help organisations implement the Model Framework.

11. The guide was developed in close consultation with the industry, with contributions from over 60 organisations across the globe.

12. These include Microsoft and Suade Labs who are here with me on the panel today, as well as other established industry partners such as DataRobot, DBS Bank, KPMG, Google, Mastercard, Salesforce, and Visa.

13. This guide will pave the way for future peer assessment. Professionals who are proficient in AI governance could use the ISAGO to guide organisations in implementing the Model Framework or assess the organisations' implementation.

Second Edition of the Model Framework

14. Secondly, we continue to enhance the Model Framework to keep pace with rapid developments in AI. The second edition is enhanced with real-world, practical examples of how organisations have implemented the Model Framework. It also includes additional considerations for responsible AI deployment, such as robustness and reproducibility. It is the result of extensive consultation with industry and governments internationally.

15. Today, 15 organisations globally have taken up or aligned themselves to the Model Framework.

Compendium of Use Cases

16. In fact, together with these organisations, we are also releasing a Compendium of Use Cases to complement the Second Edition of the Model Framework and ISAGO. These Use Cases demonstrate how various organisations across different sectors — big and small, local and international — have implemented or aligned their practices with the Model Framework. This adoption demonstrates the relevance and practicality of the Model Framework for organisations deploying AI.

17. We believe that these three AI governance initiatives will be of interest and practical value to companies looking to deploy AI.

18. These three interlinked publications are Singapore's continuous contribution to global AI discourse and developments on AI ethics and governance.

19. We look forward to engaging more like-minded partners, as we work collectively to strengthen the model for AI-related policies and standards.

20. This work, we believe, will pave the way for the next bound in global digital economy developments by fostering trust and strengthening collaboration between public and private sectors and also with all other stakeholders.

21. Thank you again for joining me today.

Index

H

I

L

M

N

P

Q

R

S

Singapore University of Social Sciences - World Scientific Future Economy Series

(Continued from page ii)

Blockchain and Smart Contracts: Design Thinking and Programming for FinTech
Lo Swee Won, Wang Yu and David Lee Kuo Chuen

Inclusive Disruption: Digital Capitalism, Deep Technology and Trade Disputes
David Lee Kuo Chuen and Linda Low

www.ingramcontent.com/pod-product-compliance
Ingram Content Group UK Ltd.
Pitfield, Milton Keynes, MK11 3LW, UK
UKHW022103170926
8624IPUK00024B/42

9 789811 218958